(417)865-5408

Run, Chicken, Run

Run, Chicken, Run

James L. Eakins

Ozarks' Good News
Ozark, Missouri

Unless otherwise indicated, all scriptural quotations are from the *King James Version* of the Bible. © 1982 by Thomas Nelson, Inc.

Run, Chicken, Run
Published by:
Ozarks' Good News
P.O. Box 825
Ozark, MO 65721
ISBN 0-9714763-0-6

Cover design and book production by:
Double Blessing Productions
P.O. Box 52756, Tulsa, OK 74152
www.doubleblessing.com

Printed in the United States of America.

Dedication

The author dedicates this book in loving memory of: Guy and Martha Jane Eakins: his remarkable, loving parents and to four wonderful people whose lives were cut short:

Galen Dale Eakins — his brother.

Tonya Louise Eakins — his niece.

J. L. Bennett — his brother-in-law.

Melvin L. Patterson — a good friend.

Contents

Acknowledgments

I am very grateful for Janet Bunn, who wrote the introduction to this book. She also was kind enough to read the entire text, chapter by chapter, as it was being written. My thanks are also offered to Jim and Connie Belknap, who worked endlessly in proof reading and typing. A big thanks to my wonderful wife, Judy, who has given many helpful suggestions. Also, Dan Sandoval, my good friend, who was kind enough to write this book's forward. Finally, I want to express my appreciation to the congregation of the Ozark Full Gospel Church, of which I am currently pastor. Their encouragement and support will long be remembered.

Foreword

The Bible. This is a statement that sums up this book. No, this is not a replacement, or translation of the Bible; it is a book filled with sermons and stories that are all about one thing. That one thing is the Bible.

Often there are those who try to run from Christian material; however, you will find this to be a very interesting book. It is filled with easy to read messages that are simple, yet minister to your soul in a very powerful way that only sermons based on the Word of God can do.

Many of the sermons in this book have been read by thousands of readers in a monthly publication called the Ozarks' Good News, of which I am the editor. I receive letters from people across America who have thoroughly enjoyed these sermons and have told of how their lives were changed.

These sermons will draw you closer to God, fill your heart with love through the Holy Spirit, and above all, reveal to you the saving knowledge of Jesus Christ.

—*Daniel L. Sandoval*

Introduction

It is both an honor and a pleasure for me to write the introduction to this book. *Run, Chicken, Run* is a long-overdue collection of some of the best of James Eakins' sermons, newspaper articles, and poems. It is filled with stories that will touch your heart and tickle your funnybone.

I have known James for nearly two decades, as an evangelist, a pastor, a missionary, newspaper publisher, and as senior administrator of the Christian school where I am the principal. James is the pastor of Ozark Full Gospel Church, where I am a charter member, and I am privileged and blessed to hear him preach several times every week.

James is the proud and loving father of eight children. He has been married for twenty-six years to his partner in ministry, Judy, who is more like the Proverbs 31 wife than any woman I've ever known. It is because of Judy that James is able to devote his whole-hearted attention to the ministry, and that he does. Like Jabez in the Bible, he is constantly asking God to enlarge his territory so that more of his word will get out, and more people will come to the Lord. His only hobby is fishing, and occasional trips to the river with his sons are treasured times in his life. Many of his favorite fishing stories are included in this book, and have led to poignant insights about our relationship with God. As much as he loves to fish, he will tell you, without a doubt, that fishing for men is even better.

James began preaching shortly after his salvation in 1978. As God opened doors, he preached in a number of churches in southwest Missouri. His first pastorate was the McCord Bend Southern Baptist Church, followed by Wheelerville Union Church, and New Life Fellowship in Crane, Missouri. Then God began to burden him for missions, and he spent some time preaching in Latin America and in the West on Indian reservations. He eventually pastored a church on the Paiute Indian Reservation at Pyramid Lake, Nevada. From there he went to Gardnerville, Nevada, where he held credentials with the Assemblies of God. Some of the messages in this book were first preached in Gardnerville. In 1994, God put a longing in James' heart to return to his hometown of Ozark, Missouri, and that fall Ozark Full Gospel Church was chartered.

I first met James when he came to the tiny Ozark community of Wheelerville, Missouri, where he began to pastor a little country church. It was there that I witnessed the sparks ignite, which soon became a blazing fire of revival sweeping through that countryside, and changed innumerable lives for all eternity. The Wheelerville Union Church was overflowing, and an old-fashioned brush arbor church was built on a corner of my family's farm in the summer of 1985. Many people today have never experienced worshipping God in an outdoor tabernacle, with a ceiling made of brush and the stars peeking through, side walls consisting only of strategically placed, rough-hewn timbers of sturdy oak, and a floor of mowed grass, dirt, and some wood shavings. But let me tell you, it doesn't take a stained-glass cathedral for God to conduct business. Anywhere an anointed man of God delivers fresh manna from Heaven to a hungry people, you are likely to see the glory of God manifested, and people's lives touched and transformed. Such was the case that summer many years ago, when night after night, James Eakins brought the word of the Lord, like hot bread fresh out of God's oven, to all who would receive it. I saw many of my friends and neighbors make their way to old wooden altars, where they wept and cried out to God, and gave their hearts to Jesus, and then returned on the nights following with their sisters, brothers, children, cousins, and friends so they, too, could find food for their souls, and new life in Christ. The messages were straightforward and to the point, preached without apology or hesitation from the pages of the King James Bible, yet tinged with the wit and wisdom of the Ozarks.

As I read through this manuscript, the memories of that brush arbor revival became vivid in my mind. Although most of these sermons are of more recent origin, I believe they all have roots that go back to those days. Some of the messages contained in this book are very pointed—as the Bible says, "sharper than any two-edged sword". But if I were needing a heart transplant, I wouldn't want the surgery done with a butter knife. My prayer is that if you need a brand new heart, this book will be an instrument in the hand of the Master Surgeon, who is both well able and more than willing to perform such an operation.

Maybe you, like me, received a new heart from Jesus many years ago, but you find the ground in that heart has become a little hardened and stony. Let God use this book to do some plowing, planting, fertilizing, and watering so that you will blossom and produce the fruit that the Lord intends for you to bring forth.

— Janet Bunn

Often, there are those who try to run from Christian material.

However, you will find this is a very interesting book.

If you don't want to be blessed, then drop this book and run.

But if you're not afraid of God's blessings, read on.

Run, Chicken, Run

Uh, Oh! Here Comes Trouble!

It's been said that children are like mosquitoes— when the bugging stops, and everything gets quiet, the trouble is about to begin. On a Sunday afternoon, several years ago while pastoring in the state of Nevada, I began making my way from the church parsonage to our main auditorium. I came around the corner of my house, and found two of my little children sitting and playing in the middle of the walkway. They had managed to get dirt and gravel all over themselves and the sidewalk. When the two boys looked up and saw me coming, they knew they were caught, and both cried in unison, "Uh, oh! Here comes trouble!"

Sometimes, I think it's amazing who we think the troublemakers are. Adam and Eve might have said as God approached the garden, "Uh, oh! Here comes trouble." Cain, with the blood of Abel, his brother, still dripping from his fingers might have said, "Uh, oh! Here comes trouble!" Those who laughed and mocked Noah, as the storm clouds began to thunder, might have said, "Uh, oh! Here comes trouble!" As Moses came near Pharaoh's palace, and the Nile River began to turn to blood, King Pharaoh might have said, "Uh, oh! Here comes trouble!" As the children of Israel were worshipping the golden calf, and Moses began to descend off Mount Sinai, they might have said, "Uh, oh! Here comes trouble!"

The Psalmist in Psalm 77:3 cried, "I remembered God, and was troubled." So many times when we have to face difficulties, our hearts are troubled, and the worst trouble of all is when we find ourselves out of harmony with God. Many times we are tempted to think others are our problem. Rather than change our own ways, we even blame God.

The sweetest thing a heart can ever experience is finding delight in God. Psalm 104:33 shouts, "I will sing unto the Lord as long as I live." Verse 34 declares, "My meditation of him shall be sweet: I will be glad in the Lord." Okay, be honest. Who is the trouble-maker, anyway? We all know it can't be God. Look, I know others can be a lot of trouble, but if you will just turn right and go straight, your meditation of God can be sweet.

As I conclude this little mind bender, let me give you some right turns to take.

First: Turn away from sin.

Second: Turn to Jesus Christ. He alone can forgive your sin debt.

Third: Turn away from everything you are doing wrong, and make things right. Then keep going straight. God will give you his mercy and power in Jesus' name.

If you keep having trouble, keep going straight to God in prayer, and he will help you through the maze.

Have You Been Pushing all the Wrong Buttons?

I remember the first microwave that was introduced into our home. John, one of my brothers, just would not eat anything prepared in it. He said, "I don't want to glow in the dark." I recall the first time I used it. I was going to bake a small potato. I began pushing buttons. It wasn't long until I discovered I was in a heap of trouble. You just don't heat a little potato ninty-nine minutes in a microwave. Not only that, this microwave was Mom's brand new toy, and woe be unto me if I messed it up. In desperation, I tried everything. I even succeeded in changing the temperature and the clock, but I still had a little spud facing ninty-nine minutes of high tech lightning. Then I heard it— the dreadful sound of Mom's footsteps headed for the kitchen. Just as Mom arrived, I saw it. There it was: the "all clear" button. With a quick push I beeped my big mess away.

Help from Above

Today, rescue workers hear the cry, "Help" coming from a burning building. Again, the cry comes from a raging, roaring river, "Help! I'm drowning." Then, out of mangled steel on a bloody highway, a terrified voice pleads, "Help" from the wreckage of an automobile. Once again, the painful cry comes from an operating room, "Help." Then again, hanging from a jagged cliff, an exhausted man, holding frantically to a little twig, screams for help. Today, the cry for help spiritually is just as real as the cry for help from those who dial 9-1-1. Thank God, there is help from above. In the book of Hebrews 4:16, you can find what I call the "help" verse of the Bible. Listen to what it says about God's throne, "Let us therefore come boldly unto the throne of grace, that we may obtain mercy, and find grace to help in time of need." God's 9-1-1 is Hebrews 4:16. In this verse you can find God's emergency care.

I would like for you to notice three beautiful things about God's throne. Here they are. First, God's throne is a throne of grace to those of us who approach it in the name of Jesus Christ. Second, at God's throne we can obtain mercy through the shed blood of Christ. Third, there is help in the time of need for all of us who come boldly to God's throne. Just think about grace, mercy, and help. Mercy will take care of the past. Grace will take care of the future. Mercy points backwards. Grace points forward to all of our future needs. Mercy covers a multitude of sins, and helps deliver us over and over again.

A story is told of D.L. Moody, one of the great preachers of yesterday. One day in the city of Chicago, he was consumed with the desire to share God's love. He ran out on the busy sidewalk, and began to cry out, "Hey, have you found her? Hey, have you found her?" And of course someone replied, "Found who?" With that, Mr. Moody replied, "Grace, have you found the grace of God, yet?" That was his opportunity to share God's true feelings for sinful man. Praise God! By God's grace, I'm going to Heaven; and because of his mercy, I've been forgiven of sin. Just thinking about the punishment Jesus took on my behalf makes me shout and cry. I cry because he suffered, and shout because he is the propitiation for our sins, and not for ours only, but also for the sins of the whole world. The word "propitiation" simply means our Holy God is now made happy through the shed blood of Christ.

Mercy — what a wonderful gift! Another story is told of a young man who had committed a terrible crime. As he approached the judge, the judge noticed he was uneasy, and very frightened. The judge replied, "Son, don't worry. You will get justice in my court." Then the young man cried, "Please, sir, I don't want justice, I want mercy!" Now look, Jesus satisfied the justice of God the Father so that we could obtain mercy, and find grace to help in the time of need. So please remember, whether you're in trouble physically or spiritually, God has a 9-1-1, too. It is Hebrews 4:16,

> **So let us therefore come boldly unto the throne of grace, that we may obtain mercy, and find grace to help in the time of need.**

Don't forget God's throne is a throne of grace, mercy and help. So when tragedy strikes, look up and cry, **"Help!"**

Have you been pushing all the wrong buttons? Then I have some good news for you. Remember the microwave? God has an 'all clear' button, too. It's found in 1 John 1:9.

> **If we confess our sins, he is faithful and just to forgive us our sins, and to cleanse us from all unrighteousness.**

Is your life all messed up? Then push the all clear button. Why don't you, right now, open your heart to God's wonderful plan for your life. Confess your sins to Jesus Christ. My friend, on the authority of God's word, when you turn away from sin to trust the Lord Jesus Christ, all the past shall be forgiven and forgotten. *Then you can say,"All clear, I'm now like an airplane ready for take off."*

Let's read these words spoken by John the Baptist in John 1:29,

> **The next day John seeth Jesus coming unto him, and saith, Behold the Lamb of God, which taketh away the sin of the world.**

Thank God we have an "all clear" button. Jesus not only shed his blood and died for us, he also paid our sin debt, and God the Father expressed his approval of Holy Jesus by raising him from the dead. So today, Jesus the Son of God, has all power to save us from our deadly sins. God has made available to us an "all clear" button so that when we do discover we have been pushing all the wrong buttons, we can look to Jesus and live. Right now, push your broken down heart to Jesus.

I. Will Later

Found Dead in Christian County

First of all, I would like to say that this sermon idea was not created by me. I received this idea from the late Pastor Jack Hudson of Charlotte, North Carolina.

I recall some years ago, a five-year-old boy became lost in the woods. As night drew near, the daddy and mommy were frantic. Many others joined them in the search for the little boy. Snow began to fall, hindering the search. Despite their searching, little Jimmy could not be found. The next morning the weary father, having looked all night, decided to return home. While walking, he gently kicked what seemed to be a log lying across the pathway. Suddenly, the snow covered bundle moved, a small boy stretched, yawned, sat up, and said, "Oh, Daddy, I've found you at last." *Did you know God is looking for you?* Oh, he knows where you are. Still, he is eagerly looking for you to turn completely to him.

I'm shocked at the hundreds of people who have good intention to give their life to God, but they never do. *May you be found alive before it's too late!*

I. Will Later of Ozark, Missouri, was found dead from injuries sustained in a tragic event. Mr. Later was employed at the Too Busy Factory in Wantmore,

Missouri. He was a member of the Social Church, where he attended one time. The cause of death has not been completely determined. I. Will Later was the son of Some Day Later, and Hopefully Later of Springfield, Missouri. Survivors at this moment include his wife, May B. Later of Ozark, Missouri. Three sisters, I. May Later of Sparta, Missouri, Hope To Later of Nixa, Missouri, and I. Shall Later of Rogersville, Missouri. Three brothers, Going To Later of Ava, Missouri, I'll Try Later of Chadwick, Missouri, and I Can Later of Spokane, Missouri. I. Will has successfully ruined one son, I. Will Later, Jr. of No Hope, Missouri, and a host of other procrastinating relatives and friends.

Funeral services may be held sooner than many of you think. I. Will Later will be buried, and eventually forgotten at the "Anyone Can Die Graveyard." Today he has found his eternal unrest at the great judgment. We do want to extend a thank you to all the pallbearers. They are as follows: Sooner Or Later, Some Time Later, Not Now But Later, I Might Later, and Someone Will Later. Honorary Pallbearers are as follows: Cousin I'm Not Religious, and Uncle Too Busy. Mr. Later shall be missed by all.

I know that many of you who are reading this obituary have plans some day to make peace with God. However, you only have this moment guaranteed. *Remember,*

> **And as it is appointed unto men once to die, but after this the judgment.**
>
> **Hebrews 9:27**

Please take a moment to fill out the following form. This form will help the preacher conduct your funeral. Please fill in the words. If I die today, I will go to H________. If you can't answer, or you don't like your answer, please give your life to Jesus Christ immediately.

If you were deathly sick, would you send for a doctor *tomorrow*? If your house caught fire, would you call the fire department *tomorrow*? If you were severely injured, would you call an ambulance *tomorrow*? Of course not! But man can sometimes be so foolish in the things that concern his soul. It's sad, but man will go on banking on his tomorrows until his account is empty, and his soul has been destroyed.

Remember, God loves you.

For God so loved the world, that he gave his only begotten son, that whosoever believeth in him should not perish, but have everlasting life.

For God sent not his son into the world to condemn the world; but that the world through him might be saved.

John 3:16,17

Have I Got a Fish Story for You

My daddy told me a humorous story years ago about a man who always seemed to bring home a boat load of fish. It was amazing, and people wondered how he could be so successful. The game warden heard of this man's great success, and asked to go with him. The two men started early one morning, and went across the lake to a secluded area. The warden noticed that the fisherman did not have a fishing pole, just a net, and a rusty old tackle box.

When they got to the appointed place, the fisherman opened the box, pulled out a stick of dynamite, lit it, and tossed it into the river. It blew up, and the fish floated to the surface. The fisherman began dipping his net into the water, and putting the fish into the boat. The warden revealed from his hip pocket the credentials of a game warden! Calmly, the fisherman opened the tackle box again, got out another stick of dynamite, lit the fuse, and handed it to the game warden. Then, as the fuse burned down, the fisherman asked, "Are you going to fish, or are you just going to sit there?"*

A few months ago, I took some time to take my children fishing. I must confess, I had a great time. My schedule usually keeps me going day and night with very little time to relax, but despite my busy schedule, we caught some really nice fish, and enjoyed a boatload of fun. As I was watching my boys fish, my mind went back about thirty-five years ago, when my daddy took me fishing. Now just like any fisherman (or exaggerator), I have some really great fishing stories. But I'll not bore you with mine. However, my dad told me a story that I have never forgotten. Here is how it unfolded:

My dad had two other fishing buddies by the name of Ike and Leo. One day these two guys got mad, and stopped talking to each other. However, being fishing buddies, they still went fishing together with my dad. These two guys had not said a word to each other for days. A few minutes after arriving at the river, the two mad buddies, in their silence, began to fish. All of a sudden, Ike hooked a big catfish. My dad said, "My, that's a big fish. What do you think, Leo?" Leo didn't say a word. Nothing could get him to speak. Then again Ike caught another even bigger fish. My dad, once again with an excited voice said, "That is a really nice fish. Leo, look at that fish!" Leo didn't say a word. He was still mad. It was obvious that these two buddies were headlocked in their silence. All of a sudden Ike shouted, "I got him, I got him." It looked like he had hooked the biggest fish in the river. Then my dad said, "Leo, look at that!" Leo didn't say a word. He just reached into his pocket, pulled out his pocket knife, opened it up, reached over, and cut Ike's fishing line. Well, the fight was on, and the silence was broken. Ike said, "Leo, why did you cut my line?" Leo replied, "Because you were having too much fun." Well, you can imagine what happened on the river bank. My dad told me that years later, these two buddies would tell this story, and laugh until they could laugh no more.

Now after hearing this story, I marvel how well things turned out for these two buddies. *I know some fishermen who would never have forgiven Leo for his pocket knife vengeance.* Unforgiveness often means we desire to hurt the people who have wounded us. It's like the little boy who was sitting on a park bench in obvious agony. A man walking by asked him, "What's wrong?" The boy answered, "I'm sitting on a bumble bee." Then the man asked, "Why don't you get up?" The boy replied, "Because, I figure I'm hurting him more than he is hurting me!"

The healing process begins when we get off the park bench. God will only heal our wounds when we stop inflicting pain upon the one who hurts us. *If we don't let God heal our wounds from the past, those hurts will turn into hate. The seed of unforgiveness will sprout into the root of bitterness (Hebrews 12:15), and the hurt we submerge within us will become a land mine. Then when someone places the slightest pressure on our area of hurt, we explode!* Something happens to our anger after we keep it for more than one day. It becomes repressed, and pushed down into the soil of our hearts. This two-day-old anger then turns into the seed of unforgiveness. After we nurture the seed of unforgiveness in the soil of our hearts, it sprouts into the root of bitterness.

> **Looking diligently lest any man fail of the grace of God; lest any root of bitterness springing up trouble you, and thereby many be defiled.**
>
> **Hebrews 12:15**

Let us remember from the bloody cross of Calvary, Jesus cried, "Father, forgive them; for they know not what they do," Luke 23:34. Of course, the first principle of forgiveness for us is this: we cannot give away something we haven't first received. So our first prayer must be, "God, be merciful to me a sinner!" Luke 11:2-4 tells us to pray,

> **...Our Father which art in Heaven, Hallowed be thy name. Thy kingdom come. Thy will be done, as in heaven, so in earth.**
>
> **Give us day by day our daily bread.**
>
> **And forgive us our sins; for we also forgive every one that is indebted to us. And lead us not into temptation; but deliver us from evil.**

My friend, why don't you turn your whole life around? You can do this by making peace with God.

> **This then is the message which we have heard of him, and declare unto you, that God is light, and in him is no darkness at all.**
>
> **If we say that we have fellowship with him, and walk in darkness, we lie, and do not the truth:**
>
> **But if we walk in the light, as he is in the light, we have fellowship one with another, and the blood of Jesus Christ his Son cleanseth us from all sin.**
>
> **If we say that we have no sin, we deceive ourselves, and the truth is not in us.**
>
> **If we confess our sins, he is faithful and just to forgive us our sins, and to cleanse us from all unrighteousness.**
>
> **1 John 1:5-9**

Fishing is Daddy's Work, Too!

Dad, it's been a long, long time since you and I fished this river;
Yet in my heart, sweet times
I'll always remember.
Memories of crackling fire,
And hot coffee as thick as tar;
The smell of worms and fish upon my hands,
And in my shoes, the river's sand.
A fly rod in your hand, and a bucket of minnows,
It's time for you to fish the willows.
"Quiet, my son," you would always say,
"Fishing is work! Not just play."
Dad, every time, I know not how,
You'd catch that big one,
And I would say — "Wow!"
My, this little boy sure did like to fish;
But Dad, to see you catch a big one
was always my wish.

Now I'm grown, and the memories of you flood my soul;
And at this river my emotions are out of control.
For standing beside me is my son;

Same river; same spot, where you and I
had so much fun.
Dad, this river still runs deep,
And the fishing here is ever so sweet.
Dad, you've been dead a long, long time;
And a greater man I will never find.
So let me say, on this Father's Day;
Dad, you were right!
Fishing is work, not just play.

Written on Father's Day
June 18, 2000
By: Pastor James L. Eakins

Can You Sleep on a Stormy Night?

Late one afternoon a wearied mother sent her little boy to bed. She heard him grumbling to himself, "Every time she gets tired, I'm the one who ends up having to go to bed!" I don't suppose there is anything more boring to a little child than being made to take a nap.*

I recall one time, my brother and I were engaged in one of those boring nap times. As brothers will do, we decided to have a pillow fight. With pillows in hand, we took our stand upon the bed. I was ready for the battle. My brother didn't know I had slipped one of my older brother's boots into my pillow slip. *My brother said, "Go ahead — hit me."* So around and around, I took careful aim, and in one glorious moment I hit him right in the jaw. Talk about flipping head over heels off the bed — he just rolled. Well, you can guess what happened next. Yep, Mom took over. After that happy day, at least for me, I could never again talk my brother into another pillow fight.

Now that I am grown, I look back on that childhood moment and smile. When I was a child, I played as a child, but now that I am a man, I've put away childish things.

Today, there are times when the responsibilities of life seem unbearable. I know life's storms can be tough. Life's answers have become even more complex, and so have the questions. *How do I sleep on a stormy night? How do I keep my sanity? How do I keep peace in my mind? How do I stand when all beneath me is sinking sand?* Well, I have a simple answer, and it works.

When you can't sleep on a stormy night, and there seems to be no rest, *go ahead — have a pillow fight with the devil!* In Genesis 28, we read about a man named Jacob who, in a very troubled time in his life, found himself alone in a desert place. As the darkness began to cover him, he cleared off a spot on the barren ground. With only stones for his pillow, he slowly drifted off to sleep. Jacob received a night vision from God, and even in all of his uncertainties and fears, God revealed to Jacob his love. *God himself had slipped a spiritual rock in Jacob's pillow, and the devil couldn't win.* The devil couldn't keep Jacob down, or afraid. With great peace, Jacob arose the next morning in God's powerful love, and so can you!

Go ahead! Hit the devil right on the side of the head with your pillow of stone. Go ahead! Sing with the pure heart of a little child,

Jesus loves me! this I know,
For the Bible tells me so;
Little ones to Him belong,
They are weak but He is strong.
Yes, Jesus loves me,
Yes, Jesus loves me,
Yes, Jesus loves me,
The Bible tells me so.

Psalm 42:8 reminds us that God is always in command. The Psalmist explains God's care like this: "Yet the Lord will command his lovingkindness in the daytime, and in the night his song shall be with me, and my prayer unto the God of my life." In this promise of God, we have the pillow of comfort. This pillow has a song in it.

Psalm 41:3 says, "The Lord will strengthen him upon the bed of languishing: thou wilt make all his bed in his sickness." Did you notice the words "God will make all your bed?" That includes your pillow. God has not only slipped the eternal rock of love in your pillow, but he has put a song in it, too. *So lay your ear against your pillow, and hear the old song written by William W. Walford:*

Sweet hour of prayer! sweet hour of prayer!

That calls me from a world of care,

And bids me, at my Father's throne,

Make all my wants and wishes known;

In seasons of distress and grief,

My soul has often found relief,

And oft escaped the tempter's snare

By Thy return sweet hour of prayer.

Now, I can't help but be reminded that one day Jesus Christ himself was fast asleep on a pillow. Mark 4:38 reads, *"And he was in the hinder part of the ship, asleep on a pillow." Make no mistake, Jesus Christ could sleep on a stormy night! This is the pillow of God's protection and power.* In this story, we are told that the very ship Jesus was in was about to sink. The storm was horrendous, and the disciples were terrified. They cried out to Jesus, *"Master, carest thou not that we perish?"* Then Jesus arose from his pillow of sleep, and rebuked the wind and sea, and the storm stopped raging. *You see, Jesus had already stuffed his pillow full of the faith of God. He knew God had everything under control, and so should you.*

Why don't you, before the sun sets on your life today, begin stuffing your pillow full of God's purpose and plan for your life. Turn from your sins with all your heart to God. Ask Jesus Christ to forgive you. Quickly, while the storm clouds are still gathering, find a place to pray, and make peace with God through the blood of Jesus Christ. *Then, next time you can't sleep on a stormy night, you can have a pillow fight with the devil, and win,* because inside of your pillow of rest will be the eternal rock of God's love, music, and comfort from Heaven, the protection, and power of God.

Turn on the Lights, and Go Back to Bed

Outside, the winter storm was blowing through the Carson Valley. Our house was very dark, and very quiet, except for the storm without. Then out of my little boy's bedroom came a whisper, "Daddy, I'm scared. I can't sleep."

That night I was about to learn a very precious lesson. For I, too, was in a storm, only this storm was within my heart. To my son, I said very impatiently, "Just turn on the lights, and go back to bed. There is nothing that is going to hurt you." Then at that moment, God seemed to say to my heart, "That's good advice. Why don't you turn on the light, and go back to bed?"

Then I remembered a beautiful story recorded in the Bible. It's found in Matthew 8, Mark 4, and again in Luke 8. Standing at the seashore, Jesus said to his disciples, *"Let us pass over to the other side."* Little did his disciples know that on their way over, there would be a terrible storm. The ship would look doomed, and their lives would be in danger. What was fascinating, even in this horrifying storm, is that Jesus Christ would be fast asleep. That's when the disciples came running to Jesus, crying in terror, *"Master, Master, carest thou not that we perish?"* Then Jesus arose, and rebuked the wind saying unto the sea, *"Peace be still,"* and the wind ceased, and there was a great calm. Then, turning to his disciples, he asked, *"Where is your faith?"*

Did not Jesus say to his disciples, *"Let us pass over unto the other side*?" Wasn't the Master of the storm with them? Of course! Listen, their ship was not going down — not when Christ was with them — and your ship won't sink either. Hey, these disciples could have gone to bed like Jesus, and gotten a good night's sleep.

Now, what should have been the disciples' response in this terrifying storm? Jesus, with great disappointment asked, *"Where is your faith?"* Would great faith fight the storm? Would great faith try to change the storm? Or would great faith turn on the light of God's word, and go back to bed? Remember, Jesus was asleep on a pillow, sleeping like a baby, with total trust in his Heavenly Father. Don't forget, in the beginning Jesus said, *"Let us pass over to the other side."* After the storm, the story ends with the proclamation, *"And they arrived." Remember, there has never been a storm so big that it hasn't blown out!*

In closing, let me say to your troubled heart, great faith can turn on the light of God's love, word, and power, and allow you to go back to bed. Why not just relax right now, look to Jesus, and rest?

Be Still!

A meditation from Mark 4:39 and Psalm 46:10

When the storm rages, and the thunders roar, and everything around you is shaken.
When your heart hurts to the very core,
And it seems all peace has been taken —
Be still!

When the sounds of danger cannot be ignored,
And your life is tearfully filled.
When the pain is too great, and you cannot take more,
God's grace is sufficient —
Be still!

When your heart trembles on a black, stormy night,
And it seems that tragedy is near.
God's love will remove all your fright,
So be of good cheer —
Be still!

So look to Jesus, who is power and might,
And he will calm your fears.
For he will command in
The midst of your storm, peace —
Be still!

Has the Devil Licked the Stripes Off Your Candy Cane?

Once I heard a story told about a little boy who wandered into a candy store. While there, he looked at all kinds of enticing sweets. After a short time, his eyes fell upon a big jar of candy cherries. The store manager kept noticing that this little guy just couldn't take his eyes off the candy jar. So, the manager took off the lid and said, "Son, go ahead and get yourself a handful." The boy never moved a muscle. He just kept staring. Then the manager urged again, "Go ahead, get a handful." And again the little fellow never moved. So after a while, the store manager reached in with his big hand and pulled out a big heaping handful of juicy candy, and then filled the little boy's hands until they were running over. As the little guy began to walk away with his big load of candy, the store manager asked, "Son, why wouldn't you get your own candy?" Then a big smile came across the little fellow's face and he said, "Because, your hand is bigger than mine!"

This story reminds me that God's hand is bigger than mine, and if I'm going to have sweets for eternity they must come from God. He alone holds the whole world in his hands. When I was a little boy, I remember growing up in Ozark, Missouri. It was a tiny town. On the northeast corner of the square was a

Ben Franklin store. Everyone at that time called it the dime store. (Now I realize some towns, especially expanding communities, don't even have a town square with the court house in the middle, and stores built around it.) However, this dime store had some of the most amazing candy. Among those sweets was that old-fashioned candy cane, soft with red and white stripes. My, just looking at it made my taste buds dance. I remember the first time I got one of these big candy canes. Not only did it taste great, but the red and white stripes really looked nice. I recall licking it for a while before being intruded upon by my brother, and our old black dog who shared the candy cane with me against my will. After taking what they wanted of the treat, I noticed how something had begun to happen to my candy cane. It got sticky, and the pretty stripes disappeared. After that, old Blacky, my dog, got to take ownership of what was left of my candy. Now, let me ask you a question. *Has the devil licked the stripes off your candy cane? Is there something missing in your life?* The Bible declares in Romans 14:17, "For the kingdom of God is not meat and drink; but righteousness, and peace, and joy in the Holy Ghost."

In Matthew 6, Jesus Christ tells us life is more than just existing. This should encourage you to begin to seek God with all your heart. In Revelation 3:20, Jesus Christ declares, "Behold, I stand at the door, and knock: If any man hear my voice, and open the door, I will come in to him, and will sup with him, and he with me." Today would be a great day for you to find a place of prayer, and pour your heart out to the Lord Jesus Christ. Then in return, you will find he will fill your heart with peace, and joy. *Has the devil licked the stripes off your candy cane?* Listen — all of the thrills of this world will fade away, but the thrill of making peace with God through our Lord Jesus will never fade away.

The Awe of the Thunderstorm

One of the first things we must all admit is that the thunderstorm is one of God's most unique creations. The rolling thunder commands attention. Both in the book of Psalms, and in Isaiah, thunder is called the voice of God. The Hebrew word for thunder means "voice." Many of the Hebrews believed that thunder was the voice of Jehovah.

In Job 26:13,14, it is said of God,

> **By his spirit he hath garnished the heavens; his hand hath formed the crooked serpent.**
>
> **Lo, these are parts of his ways: but how little a portion is heard of him? but the thunder of his power who can understand?**

I would like to make four observations of the thunder:

First: There's a lot of power up there, and it is entirely independent of man. Every thunderstorm should remind us of the power of God to judge. Often, the heavens above will declare our awesome God.

Second: Thunder is an unusual noise! And it demands and inspires awe. I know of nothing more breathtaking than to watch a massive rolling thunder cloud! It possesses the skies with its awesome power. The lightning flashes, and the deep boisterous thunder sends chills up and down one's spine.

Third: Have you noticed thunder will insist that you look up. I think sometimes we tend to ignore the heavens. We become so busy we fail to look up. So, I believe sometimes the rolling thunder comes, and God says through the storm, *"Look up."* In Isaiah 45:22, God declares,

Look unto me, and be ye saved, all the ends of the earth: for I am God, and there is none else.

Fourth: When the thunderstorm gets mean, take shelter. Why? Because there is a lot of power up there, and when it comes to earth, we are no match for its fury. *By the way, we are no match for a lot of things.* That's why we need to look completely to God.

...Hear my cry, O God; attend unto my prayer.

From the end of the earth will I cry unto thee, when my heart is overwhelmed: lead me to the rock that is higher than I.

For thou hast been a shelter....

Psalm 61:1-3

The most important thing you will ever do is make Jesus Christ your shelter. It's a stormy world! *"But as for me and my house, we will serve the Lord."* I'm reminded of a small boy who was hurrying to help his mother bring the clothes in off the clothesline before the thunderstorm hit. Finally, they had gathered the last armload, and were about to close the door. The boy stood at the threshold, waved his hand at the heavens in a sweeping gesture, and said, "Okay, God ... let'er rip!"

May God keep you through every storm. Remember, there's never been a storm so big that it didn't blow out.

The Crude, Lewd, Rude, Nude Dude

There is a story in Mark 5, and also in Luke 8 about a man I call a crude, rude, lewd, nude dude. The Webster's Encyclopedia of Dictionaries makes the following definitions:

Crude — In raw state, unripe, and rough.

Rude — Uncivil and primitive.

Lewd — Obscene, indecent, and given to unlawful indulgence.

Nude — And of course this goes without saying, naked and uncovered.

Dude — A brainless dandy, a fop. (And what's a dandy? Well, sir, let's put it this way. If someone calls you a dandy, I wouldn't smile about it, and you really should quit calling your little boys dandies.)

In this account, we find a man and his demons. How many demons were there in this one man? The demons were called legion which was a term for an army. How many? Three to six thousand demons were in this one man. No wonder he had his dwelling among the tombs, and no man could bind him, no not even with chains. And always at night and day, he was in the mountains and tombs, crying and screaming like a wild animal. There in his naked state, he was exposed to every torment a man could ever imagine. In this man's sad condition there was nothing his friends could do for him; so, fearfully, they abandoned him. Then something happened. Jesus came. He came to love, and set him free from his demonic bondage. *It didn't matter that he was a crude, lewd, rude, nude dude. God loved him!* In the power of the Son of God's command, Jesus cast out every demon from this man's tortured mind and poisoned body.

The Scripture tells us the demons entered into a herd of hogs feeding near the Sea of Galilee. *About 2,000 hogs ran violently over a mountain cliff, and drowned themselves in the sea. These demons were so filthy and horrifying that not even the nasty hogs could stand their presence. I guess we could say the hogs committed hog-icide, or better yet, sooey-cide.*

Listen, I know you are not even in the least bit like this wild man, but even with all this man's troubles, Jesus was able and willing to deliver him. This miracle ends with these closing statements,

> **When they that fed them [the swine] saw what was done, they fled, and went and told it in the city and in the country.**
>
> **Then they went out to see what was done; and came to Jesus, and found the man, out of whom the devils were departed, sitting at the feet of Jesus, clothed, and in his right mind: and they were afraid.**
>
> **Luke 8:34,35**

We are told that the owners of the swine begged Jesus to go away. It was obvious that they did not like the hog-killing revival. Maybe you, too, need to sit at the feet of Jesus and be healed, or just maybe, there is a pet pig you need to let go of in your life. Sometimes people just get too attached to their nasty habits, and they just can't imagine a hog-killing revival. These unthankful swine herders are the ones who say to God, "Let go of my pig." *Conclusion? A man and his Jesus is always better than a man and his pig.* Some may even find someday their life will conclude with the epitaph, "A man, and his demons."

When we check out of this world, our true epitaph in judgment won't be a man and his job, or a man and his money, or a man and his house, it will be a man and his Jesus.

What's Bugging You Anyway?

All of us know how irritable life can become at times. There are times when a person can get so unhappy down inside that he loses sight of those things that really, truly matter.

The story is told of a scrupulous wife who tried hard to please her critical husband, but failed often. He was most cantankerous at breakfast. If she prepared scrambled eggs, he wanted poached. If she poached the eggs, he wanted them scrambled. One morning the wife poached one egg and scrambled the other, and placed the meal before him. She awaited what she thought would surely bring his unqualified approval. He stared down at the plate, and snorted, "Can't you do anything right, woman? You've scrambled the wrong egg!"*

But then again, here is a story full of sweetness. While on her honeymoon, a young bride attempted to press the trousers of her husband's new suit with an iron received as a wedding present. When she applied the hot iron, part of the trousers went up in a puff of smoke, leaving a big, ugly hole. The groom rushed in from the next room. "Is everything all right?" Whereupon the bride burst into tears, as she tried to tell what had happened. "Honey," he replied, "Let's get down on our knees, and thank God that my leg wasn't in those pants!" Isn't it sad how time and adversity can poison our attitudes?*

There is a verse of scripture that is not only a good meditation for our hearts, but it can be a medicine, too. It's found in Matthew 13:44,

> **Again, the kingdom of heaven is like unto treasure hid in a field; The which when a man hath found, he hideth, and for joy thereof goeth and selleth all that he hath, and buyeth that field.**

In this verse, God is telling us that Jesus came, and found a wonderful treasure in a field. And then he purchased the whole world with His holy blood just to get the treasure. *What is the treasure? It is men and women who will give their past, present, and future to the Lord Jesus Christ.* Notice the whole field was bought just to get the treasure. But what about the field? It's full of weeds, spiders, rats, mice, ants, bugs, thistles, rocks, and dead grass; chiggers, snakes, poison ivy and stink weeds, opossums, lizards, and stickers, awful smells, skunks, and dead things. As you walk through your field, there are bees, wasps, ants, spiders, and after a while, you discover burrs stuck to your clothes, and little bugs crawling up your legs. *But don't forget the treasure*!

I have many fond memories of my brother, Galen, who was killed in a tragic car wreck. He was a remarkable brother, and his family meant a lot to him. I remember, when I turned sixteen, and had just gotten my driver's license, Galen let me drive one of his cars. It was a five speed, Ford Cyclone, with a V8, and it would flat move. Well, I tore it all to pieces. I don't mean I wrecked it. I mean I abused it, and tore it all to pieces — even to the point, we had to tow it home. I thought my brother would kill me, but he didn't. He didn't even say a word. Galen just pulled that car into his garage, and repaired it. He never expressed one unkind word to me, or anyone else. Why? I was his little brother. He knew I was just a mixed-up kid who needed love. Do you know what else he did? He let me drive his brand new Monte Carlo the very next day. Why? Because he considered his brothers and sisters to be his treasures. Keep your eye on the treasure. Keep your mind and heart loving the things that really matter.

Here is a Small List of Things that Really Matter:

1. Our relationships, *not* accomplishments.
2. Our faith in Christ, *not* our religion.
3. Our love for one another, *not* our love for things.
4. Our children and developing Godly manners, *not* their unhealthy, fleshly pleasures.
5. Our homes, *not* our houses.
6. Our words of love, *not* our voice of complaint.
7. Our giving of our lives, *not* our self-edification.
8. Our hard work, *not* our job titles.
9. Our fruit, *not* our orchards.
10. Our future, *not* our past.
11. Our praying, *not* our playing.
12. The flowers we leave behind, *not* the weeds we let grow up.

13. Others, *not* ourselves.

14. Giving, *not* getting.

15. Our spirit that lives, *not* our flesh that dies.

16. Heaven, *not* earth.

17. Where we are going, *not* where we have been.

18. Our time that is left, *not* our time that is spent.

19. The Bread of Life, *not* the candy of pleasure.

20. The Water of Life, *not* the kool-aid of fun.

21. Things money can't buy, *not* our possessions.

22. What we are, *not* what others think we are.

I remember reading the story of a tragic house fire in Texas. When the firemen arrived, the house was already engulfed in hideous flames, and a mother was standing close to the hot flames screaming, "My God, my baby is in there, my baby is in the fire!" The firemen, knowing they had very little time if any to save the baby, asked the mother the location of her baby, and immediately one of the firemen rushed into the raging flames. In a few moments, the fireman came running out of the blackish smoke, holding a small blanket in his hand with a small object wrapped inside. The crowd around began to roar with joy, only for their shouts to be silenced by the screaming mother, as she cried at the top of her lungs, "My God, my God, you saved her dolly. It's just a doll, it's just a doll. My God, it's just her toy."

Look, I don't want to make you sad, but in the world there are a lot of horrifying things, and woe be unto us if we leave God out of our lives. *Don't forget, everyone of us has a field, and in our fields are many unpleasant things. Just remember to keep your heart and mind on the treasure. Why don't you, right now, think of some of the treasures that are in your field.* Each and everyone of them have been put in your life by God.

I want to ask you a question, "Did you know that God sees this world as a field?" This world has a lot of spiritual weeds and rocks in it, along with spiders, snakes, and a lot of other pests. However, God sees a treasure in this world, and because of it,

> **For God so loved the world, that he gave his only begotten Son, that whosoever believeth in him should not perish, but have everlasting life.**
>
> **John 3:16**

Do you want everlasting life? If you do, then present your little piece of ground to the Lord Jesus Christ. He will put treasures in your heart that will be joy unspeakable, and full of glory. *Today, turn from sin, and turn to Jesus Christ. Don't turn a little, turn completely around. Give God all your heart!* Ask Jesus to forgive you, and change your life. Then, get up and live your life for God.

Stop! Stop, You're Hurting Me!

The home is a wonderful place, a man may travel the world over in search of happiness only to return home to find it. Once I heard about a little schoolboy who went home with a pain in his stomach. His mom said, "Well, sit down, and drink some milk. Your stomach hurts because it's empty. It will be all right when you've got something in it." Afterwards, his daddy came home from work, complaining of a bad headache. "That's because it's empty," said the little son. "You would be all right if you had something in it." Now I smile at this cute little story, and my heart agrees: 'Home is a remarkable place.' However, we all need to be very careful that we keep sweet fellowship in our homes.

Several years ago, while I was pastoring in the state of Nevada, a very dear friend of mine, Ron Hathhorn was preaching to a gentleman about his need for God. Suddenly, the gentleman cried, *"Stop, stop, you're hurting me."*

Now as we think about this man's response, our consideration could go a thousand places. These words instantly make one think of someone being treated unkindly. For just a few moments, I would like to suggest these possibilities.

First: Our very own loved ones sometimes hurt needlessly.

Second: Sometimes you hurt.

Third: Don't forget, God can hurt, too.

Someone has very beautifully said, *"Love wasn't put in your heart to stay. Love isn't love until you give it away."*

In this busy rat-race of ours, there is a great concern in my heart for the family. I'm reminded of the great hymn, *Love Lifted Me*, written by James Rowe. The chorus goes like this: *Love lifted me! Love lifted me! When nothing else could help, Love lifted me.* Do you need a lift? Does your family need a lift? Have you forgotten the greatest joy of all? You know it is the expression of love. It doesn't matter whether you're rich or poor, love is a gift to all. There are a thousand things you could do without money to enjoy your family, and lift their spirits.

I think so many times we get captured by the frustrations of everyday life, and lose sight of what is best for our homes. Proverbs 17:22 says, "A merry heart doeth good like a medicine: but a broken spirit drieth the bones." It has been proven that laughter causes the sick to mend. *So let's keep it upon our hearts, joy in the home is a must.* Let us never forget love needs to be expressed daily. Don't fight and fuss. *Stop, stop, you're hurting them. Many of the tears in your home are completely unnecessary.* Remember, First Corinthians 13 teaches us that love is patient and kind, love is not jealous, or conceited, or proud; love is not ill-mannered, or selfish, or irritable. Love does not keep a record of wrongs; love is not happy with evil, but is happy with truth. Love never gives up. Its faith, hope, and patience never fail. Love is eternal.

I know sometimes you hurt, too. But really, you don't have to take it out on those you love. You don't need to always have your way. You can kill a mouse with a broom, or even a rolled-up newspaper. You can also kill a mouse with a hand grenade. But if you do, you not only get the mouse, you'll get the house! Why don't you just forget the mouse for now, and love your house?

Some men were arguing about how to kill a hog. Several suggestions were made. Then finally, one man convinced them to tie two sticks of dynamite around the hog's head, and ignite it. Another argued that more dynamite was needed, but finally they settled on just the two sticks. Attaching a long fuse, they got far enough away so as not to be hurt from the explosion, and a few seconds after the fuse was lit, the dynamite exploded, and the hog completely disappeared. They couldn't even find one of its ears. The man who argued for the four sticks of dynamite rather than the two said, "I told you we should have used more dynamite! You see, he got away!"

Listen, I know you are hurt, too, but you don't have to take it out on everyone else. Stop, stop, you're hurting them.

Now, how about God? Psalm 127:1 declares,

> **Except the Lord build the house, they labour in vain that build it: except the Lord keep the city, the watchman waketh but in vain.**

Next time you are driving, or riding in your automobile, when you come to an intersection, stop, look up to your right, and you'll find a bright red octagon sign. It reads: S-T-O-P. Now always remember: S - inning T - urns O - ff P - ower! Remember the gentleman I mentioned at the beginning? He cried, "Stop, stop, you're hurting me!" Sometimes the truth stings. When you reject God's truth, you break God's heart. Has the power of joy and communication gone out at your house? If it has, I think you know where the switch is. Get everyone you love in church, and under God's tender loving care.

Stop, stop, you're hurting not only those you love and yourself, but God, too. God's love is immutable, unchangeable, as with God himself. There is in it no shadow of turning. A sinner may go to Hell unsaved, but he cannot go to Hell unloved. The Christian rejoices, and partakes in God's unending love.

Why don't you take what you've just read, and then take great courage that the one thing the devil can never steal is your opportunity to love those you call family and friends.

Putting the Graveyard Out of Business

A little girl returned from Sunday School class, and was asked by her momma what she had learned from the Easter Sunday message. The daughter excitedly retold the whole story. She told about the death of Jesus, and how he was buried in a grave. Later an angel came, looked inside the tomb, and asked Jesus what he wanted. "I want out of this hole," Jesus said. Well this little girl no doubt had her own interpretation to the Easter message, but I love it!*

As a family watched the Easter story on television, one of the children was deeply stirred. As Jesus was tortured and killed, tears rolled down her cheeks. She was absolutely silent until after Jesus had been taken down from the cross, and put into the tomb. *Then she shouted, "Now comes the good part!" We first hear about the sufferings, and death of Jesus. Now comes the good part! The tomb is empty!* **Jesus is risen from the dead!**

This year the world needs the Easter message more than ever. In fact, for you and me this ought to be the most important Easter we have ever known. After all, there are more dead people than ever before. I am not speaking now about the graveyard business, and the ever consuming graves. *I am speaking about the living dead. Those who breathe and move and walk the sidewalks, but are indifferent to God and his commands. The dropouts, the cop-outs, the sick-outs, the fall-outs, and all the others who have given up on life to live an empty existence.* Somewhere I read about a man who sat in front of a bad television program, and didn't know that he was bored. He joined the rat race of life, where personal worth was measured in terms of what he possessed, and was not aware of his anxieties, only to find bleeding ulcers spoke louder than words.

For years, philosophers have been foolishly saying God is dead, but what we see and feel now is the sickening possibility that man is dead. He's been transformed into a hideous, infectious fleshy thing — a coveting, lusting, idolater of material possessions and pleasures. There are more of these living dead men today than ever before. The covetousness of man is growing at a rapid rate. When a man lives for his own selfish pleasures, he loses sight of what really matters. Today a person is just a number. When we add to this man's personal sinful secrets and burdens of life, this just could be our most important Easter of all. Why? Because we all have an opportunity to bring our troubles and stresses to Easter's most glorious celebration. Easter is for now! Easter is, *"Jesus Christ,"* conqueror of the grave, *"...the same yesterday, today and forever."* Hebrews 13:8.

So if you have made a miserable mess of your life, remember Easter is far more than just a message of life beyond the grave. Easter is life now! It speaks to our worries and anxieties. This wonderful day calls us to a more victorious living day by day. Easter is the assurance of a living Savior. It has a special message for those who have failed. Our failure need not be final, for God never gives up on us, and His love never says farewell. Let us not ever forget the eternal words of Jesus, recorded in Revelation 1:18,

> **I am he that liveth, and was dead; and, behold, I am alive for evermore, amen; and have the keys of Hell and of death**

Turn from death today! Will you take warning today? If so, I beg you today to turn your heart from the ways of sin, seek Jesus, and find him today! God's arms of mercy are open to every penitent sinner. You may turn to Christ this moment, trust him for forgiveness and cleansing, give him your heart forever, and have everlasting life now. In Jesus' name, do it!

> **For the wages of sin is death; but the gift of God is eternal life through Jesus Christ our Lord.**
>
> **Romans 6:23.**

> **Repent, and be baptized everyone of you in the name of Jesus Christ for the remission of sins, and ye shall receive the gift of the Holy Ghost.**
>
> **Acts 2:38**

May God help you get out of the hole you're in today. Remember, Jesus put the tomb out of business. He can put your sin out of business, too. Someday he will put the graveyard out of business, also.

Oh Grave, Your Silence Doesn't Fool Me

Written standing at my Father's grave early
Easter morning as the sun began to rise.

Don't let the silence fool you, *Grave.*
For the voice of God, you must behave.
Your quietness is but for a moment,
For the trumpet shall sound, and you shall know it.

For up from your prison your captives shall rise,
To behold Jesus with brand new eyes.
Oh, Grave, your silence brings no despair,
For on resurrection morning, the saints will all be there.
My loved ones will be there in that sun shining bright,
For their creator has at last removed the night.
For in Jesus Christ their love and faith forever stands,
For the one they await will have nail prints in his hands.
Oh, Grave, your darkness carries no fright,
For Jesus has given to them all Heaven's light.
There's coming a moment, I know not when,
When all your dead silence shall come to an end.
Rocks and dirt, that's all you are,
God's power outweighs you by far.
Look up, Oh, Grave, in your darkness of night,
For in the heavens is a Morning Star bright.
For within the redeemed is the earnest of light,
For they know it's not by their power, but by God's might.
So, go ahead, Grave! Argue with your quietness of sod,
Faith, hope, and love need only the voice of God.
Oh, Grave, remember some time ago,
The dead body of Jesus you had to let go,
For up from your dead silence Christ did arise,
To return some day to claim his prize.

Like a flash in the heavens, the saints will descend,
To watch their graves come to an end.
For the Lord himself shall descend from heaven with a shout,
And at that moment, their brand new bodies shall come out.
Then, Grave, once again as in the days gone past,
You'll find yourself surprised, and beaten at last.

Written by:
Pastor James L. Eakins
April 4, 1999

There's a Bomb on the Bus

A few years back I heard about a young man by the name of Jim attending Bible college. He was there preparing for the pastorate. At the close of the semester his professor had instructed his class to prepare a sermon, and submit it with their final exam. The score for this message was very important. The day came with the results, and to Jim's disappointment, he had received an awful score. So Jim, somewhat irritated, went to the professor and said, "Why did I get such a terrible score? Wasn't the message good?" The professor said, "Jim, the message was wonderful, and everything about it was compiled to perfection." Jim cried, "Then why such a horrible score?" The professor replied, "It was your title. Who wants to hear a sermon entitled The Relativity of the Old Testament in Its Hermeneutics of the Prophets Compared to the Teachings of the Apostle Paul in Contrast to the Prophesy of the Apostle Peter?" Then the professor instructed Jim, "When you become a pastor of a church someday, you will need to have a sermon title so compelling that if a loaded Greyhound Bus was traveling by your church, as the people read the sign in front of the church, they would immediately stop, and come inside." Jim said to the professor, "Can I fix my sermon title, and get an adjusted score?" The professor replied, "Okay."

The next morning, Jim came leaping into the classroom, and laid his revised sermon on the professor's desk with its new title which read, "There is a bomb on your bus!" My, I believe that would stop a bus don't you?*

Now I know there is no bomb on your bus; at least, I hope not. *But there is a bomb ticking away in the heart of every man and woman. It's called Pressure.* This bomb is ticking away — creating stress, worry, and even fear. These pressures inside us cause everything from health problems to family strife, and will grow like a cancer into every part of one's life. Pressure is the reason for nervous breakdowns, suicide, drunkenness, drug abuse, teenage rebellion, child abuse, uncontrolled anger, divorce, fighting, hating, and the list goes on and on. Some have even tried to solve it by running away. Without a doubt this bomb called pressure is very real.

Let's look at some facts. Have you noticed everything under pressure has an outlet? For example, an electrician, when wiring a house, will always install a breaker box. This is a safety device so that when things get overloaded, it will shut down at the main source of power. If not, the house will catch fire, and burn to the ground. Then there is the car you drive. In the back of it is what the mechanic calls a tail pipe. When the car is running, if it is not expelling the fumes, it will fill with deadly poisons. Stop up the pipe completely, and it will blow something up. Let's take a look in the kitchen. Ever seen a hot, hissing, pressure cooker, or a whistling tea kettle? Stop the steam from coming out, and there is going to be a big problem in the kitchen shortly. By these three examples, it is obvious everything under pressure needs an outlet. *Pressure that kills is not something on the outside pressing in, but rather something on the inside pushing out.* Let's find a way to stop taking in more trouble than we can handle, and start finding ways of relieving the pressure that we can't stand. The only way I know how to do this is to find good, safe outlets. *Remember, all the water in the world, however hard it tried, could never sink a ship unless it gets inside.* You say, "Only one problem, I leak." So do I. No matter how hard we try, there will always be some things leaking into our hearts.

We not only must watch what we let into our hearts, but also find good healthy ways to let out the pressure. First, worry is never a good way. Worry never solved a problem, never made a home, never paid a bill, never healed the sick, never got a job, never fixed a car, never raised a child, and never calmed a storm. Someone said, "Worry is like a rocking chair. It gives you something to do, but it doesn't get you anywhere." To worry about what we can change is silly, and to worry about what we can't change is useless. Let me make a few suggestions.

Get a hold of yourself — it's going to be okay! There has never been a storm so big that it didn't blow out. Jesus said in John 14:27,"Let not your heart be troubled, neither let it be afraid." Stop right now, and take a deep breath of hope. God created you, and life is wonderful. Dear reader, worry just might be that little bit of atheism in all of us. "Okay, Preacher, how do I get a hold of myself?"

Let Jesus get a hold of you. Put Jesus where it hurts — place him in the midst of your storm — let Jesus love you in the personal areas of your heart. Jesus said in Matthew 11: 28,29

> **Come unto me, all ye that labor and are heavy laden, and I will give you rest.**
>
> **Take my yoke upon you, and learn of me; for I am meek and lowly in heart; and ye shall find rest unto your souls.**

Stop, and rest in prayer. When you stop to pray you'll be able to get your eyes off the storm, and on the peace of God. Someone said, "When you look at others, you are perplexed. When you look at yourself, you are depressed. When you look around, you are distressed, but when you look up, you are blessed."

I'm reminded of the little frog with a big smile sitting on a lily pad. A bird flew by the pond, and said to the frog, "What are you so happy about?" The little frog replied, "You'd be happy, too, if you could eat what bugs you!" Listen, there are a million and one things that bug us. But God has given unto us wonderful ways to release our pressures. Don't go the Devil's way with hate and unforgiveness, worry and strife. Don't try to solve your problems, or even ignore them by things that will only hurt you and others.

Fill Your Life with Godly Things.
Here are a Few:

Eternal life and forgiveness through Jesus Christ.

Faith and hope through the word of God (King James Version) — encouragement and fellowship in faithful church attendance — victory and power to overcome the world through the indwelling Christ, and the Holy Spirit given to all born again believers.

Prayer for rest and help.

The fruit of the Holy Spirit for a wonderful, sweet, and pleasant life, Galatians 5:22,23,

> **But the fruit of the spirit is love, joy, peace, long-suffering, gentleness, goodness, faith,**
>
> **Meekness, temperance: against such there is no law.**

To sum it all up — without God you are going to blow up. With God you can find the sweet release you need when you are under pressure.

Why Suicide?

There comes a critical time in everyone's life when death seems to be the only escape. Experts claim that more than 85% of the population admits to having entertained suicide thoughts. It is quite possible that a person who is thinking of taking his life may be reading this book. If you are such a person, please read carefully. It may be that you think that nobody cares. You may feel hopelessly confused, be involved with alcohol and drugs, or maybe under so much pressure that you see no way out of your problems. But the honest truth is you don't really want to die. What you want is to be able to stop the pain of living, and get out of your problem. You're hurting, and nobody seems to understand, or maybe you have hid everything inside, and at this moment you can't imagine a time when the hurting will stop. Although you may find it hard to believe, your problems will lessen and, in time, they will clear up.

Hang on! You are Stronger Than You Think

Please remember one important thing — killing yourself is a permanent solution to a temporary problem. Thinking about suicide can become very, very dangerous, especially when a method is available, and you have planned where, and when to die.

From your point of view, you have tried and failed at all the alternatives. The biggest tragedy of a suicide death is that a suicidal state of mind is temporary. *If you can just hang on, and keep yourself safe, the spirit of suicide will pass. Resist the spirit of suicide with the Spirit of God.* (Ref: Ephesians 6:12, Galatians 5:19-21, II Timothy 1:7)

There is another aspect of suicide that many do not consider. Suicide does not stop the problems. The general idea of suicide is that death will end the problem, that it will all be over. The truth is, however, when one's body dies, his soul lives on. Whether lost or saved, a person's situations do not stop with death. Once death occurs, there will be no escaping the consequences of your life, and the decisions made during it. Those who are not Christians, those who have not trusted the Lord Jesus as their personal Savior, will begin experiencing an eternal torment that will make all the headaches and heartbreaks of this life seem like child's play. (Ref.: Luke 16:23-26, Matthew 10:28, I Corinthians 3:17, Mark 9:43-50, Luke 12:5) Maybe you are one of the thousands of people who struggle with end-it-all thoughts. Perhaps you've tried to take your life, but did not succeed. Thank God for that.

Some of you have never thought about suicide at all. But at some point you may, and you need to be fully prepared to overcome it. The question is — why not suicide? There are some really good reasons why you should not take your life. For one, no suicide method is fool proof. Oh, you think you've got one that can't miss? Why don't you talk to the young man who put a gun under his chin, blew off practically his entire face, and survived?

Suppose you do 'succeed' in the attempt to end your life. Suicide, when it works, is final. Maybe that sounds insultingly elementary. I mention it only because so many have gotten the foolish idea that suicide is temporary. Once done, your fate is forever settled. If you do kill yourself, you will drastically change the lives of others who love you very much, and you will succeed in devastating their lives. However, in the end, you will be the biggest loser of all. (Ref.: Exodus 20:13)

Remember, my friend, your problems are temporary. They may seem now like a storm that will never blow out, but the rains will stop, the sky will brighten, the clouds will blow away, and the sunshine will reappear. *There is hope. There are people who care. Turn to them in your time of greatest need.* Talk to someone you trust. Let him or her give you wise counsel. If you feel that you don't have anyone, call us or write us. I, or one of our staff members will help. Why not suicide? You are the answer to that question. Your life is too valuable, too meaningful, too important to end it.

Why Not Suicide?

God created you and gave you life. Jesus Christ said, "I am come that they might have life, and that they might have it more abundantly." John 10:10. He knows what is needed to make your life beautiful. Open your heart to him. Talk to him. Tell him your need, and he will be your friend who loves and understands at all times. *Whatever you do, do not keep everything hidden inside. Open your heart to Jesus Christ, then find a friend. Confide in him or her, and hang on. Life really is the best choice.*

Now, as I close, I am aware of the fact that for some, your pain and despair may be beyond description. It could be that you are in a state of depression that has just completely overwhelmed you. Your condition is critical, and you just can't snap out of it. Let me give you three things to do immediately.

First — and most important: find a Bible believing Christian - one who is clean and totally void of sinful habits. Make sure this person attends a local church every week. Then let him or her talk to you about your sins. Let him tell you how you can be forgiven through the Blood of Jesus Christ, and how you can give your life totally to God. Then, let him pray for you and with you. This Christian will also want to share God's word with you, let him. God's word has the power to set you free. *God is bigger than you think! Hang on!* (Ref. Mark 10:27)

Second: find a doctor, and let him examine you. He will want to check your eating habits, and perhaps some addictions you may have. There may even be a physical problem creating some of your suicidal thoughts. If you can, find a good Christian doctor. Don't be shy to ask.

Third: don't hide your condition. Tell a friend, and let your friend know it is serious. If you feel you don't have a friend, remember, the church will always be your friend. *Find someone to do your thinking for you, and let him keep you safe.*

Hang on! God loves you more than you think. *Hang on!* Your friends will be strong for you, let them help. *Hang on!* You are stronger than you think. *Hang on!* God's power can and will deliver you. *Hang on!* God is bigger than the whole troubled world.

References of Scriptures in this Sermon:

For we wrestle not against flesh and blood, but against principalities, against powers, against the rulers of the darkness of this world, against spiritual wickedness in high places.

Ephesians 6:12

Now the works of the flesh are manifest, which are these, Adultery, fornication, uncleanness, lasciviousness,

Idolatry, witchcraft, hatred, variance, emulations, wrath, strife, seditions, heresies,

Envyings, murders, drunkenness, revellings, and such like: of the which I tell you before, as I have also told you in time past, that they which do such things shall not inherit the kingdom of God.

Galatians 5:19-21

For God hath not given us the spirit of fear; but of power, and of love, and of a sound mind.

2 Timothy 1:7

And in Hell he lift up his eyes, being in torments, and seeth Abraham afar off, and Lazarus in his bosom.

And he cried and said, Father Abraham, have mercy on me, and send Lazarus, that he may dip the tip of his finger in water, and cool my tongue; for I am tormented in this flame.

But Abraham said, son, remember that thou in thy lifetime receivedst thy good things, and likewise Lazarus evil things: but now he is comforted, and thou art tormented.

And beside all this, between us and you there is a great gulf fixed: so that they which would pass from hence to you cannot; neither can they pass to us, that would come from thence.

Luke 16:23-26

And fear not them which kill the body, but are not able to kill the soul: but rather fear him which is able to destroy both soul and body in Hell.

Matthew 10:28

If any man defile the temple of God, him shall God destroy; for the temple of God is holy, which temple ye are.

1 Corinthians 3:17

And if thy hand offend thee, cut it off: it is better for thee to enter into life maimed, than having two hands to go into hell, into the fire that never shall be quenched:

Where their worm dieth not, and the fire is not quenched.

And if thy foot offend thee, cut it off: it is better for thee to enter halt into life, than having two feet to be cast into hell, into the fire that never shall be quenched:

Where their worm dieth not, and the fire is not quenched.

And if thine eye offend thee, pluck it out: it is better for thee to enter into the kingdom of God with one eye, than having two eyes to be cast into hell fire:

Where their worm dieth not, and the fire is not quenched.

For every one shall be salted with fire, and every sacrifice shall be salted with salt.

Salt is good: but if the salt have lost his saltness, wherewith will ye season it? Have salt in yourselves, and have peace one with another.

Mark 9:43-50

But I will forewarn you whom ye shall fear: fear him, which after he hath killed hath power to cast into hell; Yea, I say unto you, fear him.

Luke 12:5

Thou shalt not kill.

Exodus 20:13

The thief cometh not, but for to steal, and to kill, and to destroy: I am come that they might have life, and that they might have it more abundantly.

John 10:10

Before the World Began

In hope of eternal life, which God, that cannot lie, promised before the world began.

Titus 1:2

As I begin, let me share with you a golf story I heard. Elijah, Jesus, and God are all playing golf on a sunny day. On the eighteenth hole, Elijah hits a drive right into the middle of a water brook. Well, Elijah takes his mantle and parts the water, walks out there, and hits the ball to the green.

Jesus is next, and on his turn he hits it onto a lily pad in the water brook. Well, Jesus just walks on top of the water, lines up his shot, and hits it to the green.

Now it's God's turn. He hits the ball towards the water brook, but before it hits the water a giant fish leaps up, and catches the ball in its mouth. Before the fish hits the water, a bird swoops down, and grabs the fish by its talons. The bird, not looking where it is going, flies into a tree, dropping the fish which drops the ball into the eighteenth hole ... scoring a hole in one!

While God the Father is doing his victory dance, Jesus leans over to him and says "Now Dad, if you're going to play like that, Elijah and I are not going to take you golfing again!"

My friend, the God of all creation has been planning your future. The rest of this sermon will be serious, and full of remarkable truth.

When we stepped into this new millennium, it was certain that thousands of years had passed away, and untold millions of people had lived on this earth. Each generation had enjoyed its own blessings, and had faced its own tragedies. Now, as archeologists dig in the ancient ruins of the past, they discover a people who lived their lives surrounded by friends and loved ones. As I look back thousands of years, I can't help but feel a sense of smallness. Then when I look at the world, and how big it is, and at the universe, my heart just sinks into utter despair, but thank God for Jesus Christ. Listen to his infallible words found in John 14:1-3,

> **Let not your heart be troubled: ye believe in God, believe also in me.**
>
> **In my father's house are many mansions: If it were not so, I would have told you. I go to prepare a place for you.**
>
> **And if I go and prepare a place for you, I will come again, and receive you unto myself; that where I am, there ye may be also. This is a wonderful promise. But for now, everyone of us has been born into a very troubled world.**

Do you know the Bible has some really good news? Here it is. *Before the world began, God knew you, and who you would become. It's true, he not only knows all about you, he loves you!*

Here are five things the Bible reveals about you before the world began:

1. Before your world began — God had, and still has, a plan for your life. 2 Timothy 1:7,9,10 reads,

For God hath not given us the spirit of fear; but of power, and of love, and of a sound mind.

Who hath saved us, and called us with an holy calling, not according to our works, but according to his own purpose and grace, which was given us in Christ Jesus before the world began,

But is now made manifest by the appearing of our Saviour Jesus Christ, who hath abolished death, and hath brought life and immortality to light through the gospel.

2. Before the world began — God knew all about you. In Jeremiah 1:5, God said to the prophet Jeremiah, "Before I formed thee in the belly I knew thee; and before thou camest forth out of the womb I sanctified thee, and I ordained thee a prophet unto the nations." In Psalm 139:14-18 we read,

I will praise thee; for I am fearfully and wonderfully made: marvelous are thy works; and that my soul knoweth right well.

My substance was not hid from thee, when I was made in secret, and curiously wrought in the lowest parts of the earth.

Thine eyes did see my substance, yet being unperfect; and in thy book all my members were written, which in continuance were fashioned, when as yet there was none of them.

How precious also are thy thoughts unto me, O God! how great is the sum of them!

If I should count them, they are more in number than the sand: when I awake I am still with thee.

3. Before the world began — God promised you eternal life, if you will turn from sin, and put all your trust and faith in the Lord Jesus Christ. In Titus 1:2 we read, "In hope of eternal life, which God, that cannot

lie, promised before the world began." Just think, before God made the mountains, valleys, rivers, lakes, or even created one blade of grass he promised you everlasting life.

4. Before the world began — God loved you! He still loves you, and He always will love you! In Jeremiah 31:3 God said, "Yea, I have loved thee with an everlasting love: therefore with lovingkindness have I drawn thee." Everlasting love did not begin the day before yesterday. God's everlasting love has always been even before time. Look at this great truth about the Christian's relationship to God, *"We love him, because he first loved us."* I John 4:19. In the words of one scholar by the name of Charles Spurgeon, "I'm sure glad God loved me before I was born, he sure wouldn't love me after I was born." Of course this is an exaggeration, because God still loves you and always will.

5. Before the world began — God provided you the Gospel of Christ, for it is the power of God unto salvation. In Romans 16:24-27 we read,

> **The grace of our Lord Jesus Christ be with you all. Amen.**
>
> **Now to him that is of power to stablish you according to my gospel, and the preaching of Jesus Christ, according to the revelation of the mystery, which was kept secret since the world began,**
>
> **But now is made manifest, and by the scriptures of the prophets, according to the commandment of the everlasting God, made known to all nations for the obedience of faith.**
>
> **To God only wise, be glory through Jesus Christ for ever. Amen.**

In First Peter 1:19,20, the Bible tells us that a sinner is forgiven, and saved by the precious blood of Jesus Christ.

> **But with the precious blood of Christ, as of a lamb without blemish and without spot: Who verily was foreordained before the foundation of the world, but was manifest in these last times for you.**

Just think, according to Psalm 139:17,18, "How precious also are thy thoughts unto me, O God! how great is the sum of them! If I should count them, they are more in number than the sand: when I awake, I am still with thee." God's thoughts of you are more in number than the sand. He even understands your thoughts afar off.

God really loves you, and he always has. Before there was ever a created world, God so loved you that he promised you eternal life. Not only did he promise, but he provided forgiveness through the death of Jesus Christ, and through the resurrection of Jesus we all can live in the redemptive power of God. So if at times you feel like a tiny little ant at the bottom of the Grand Canyon, remember before the world began, God loved you, and promised to give you eternal life through the precious blood of Christ as a lamb without blemish and without spot.

So then after all these truths, I must come to the conclusion that anyone who lives on this planet, and refuses to live for God, must be a person void of understanding. Why don't you turn from your sin today, and give your life completely to Jesus Christ? After all, Jesus died for your horrible sins so that you don't have to be lost forever. Start your Christian life now. Remember, only true Christians go to Heaven.

God Shall Make All Things New

A Meditation from Revelation 21 and 22

From the throne of God I heard a great voice
Saying, "All sorrow at last has finished its course."
Then with God's majestic shout,
"Good news, troubled earth, I'll work things out!"
"For behold, I shall make all things new.
My words are faithful, and they are true."
A brand new Heaven, with crisp blue skies,
And no demonic powers to fill it with lies.
No smog and soot to soil your majestic heights,
And no more storms will take their flights.
A new Earth I'll give unto you.
No sickness, no diseases, and no disasters, too!
No, not even a disappointment shall darken your day.
Why even the grave has vanished away,
and never again will Satan have his say.
A new holy city with streets of pure gold.
A Holy Jerusalem I'll forever bestow.
For there within its walls of clear jasper,
A new people who will only know laughter.
No tears, or sorrow, nor languishing in pain,
There a people without blemish, or shame.
For within this city my people shall reign

And in my holiness shall be their fame.
The new temple by far shall be the most glorious sight,
For I the Lord God shall be its might.
For within this city, shall be a new light,
No need of the sun, not by day or by night.
Behold, it's the Lamb of God that shines so bright,
No darkness will ever put up a fight.
A new paradise there shall forever be,
And within it a pure River of Life flowing free.
Once again a new garden of Eden
Where the serpent will never, ever get even.
For there within this garden so full of life,
Will forever grow the Tree of Life.
But woe unto you, my sinner friend,
If in this city you want in.
For if redemption hath not yet made you complete,
From the Tree of Life you never shall eat.
So quickly while there is still time,
Come to Jesus, and there forgiveness you'll find.
And then you'll hear the majestic shout,
Earth, out of your prisons you've come out.
So remember when you're down and low,
There's a better place for you to go.
For behold I shall make all things new.
These words are faithful and they are true.

Written by:
Pastor James L. Eakins
October 10, 1999

Don't Take Half a Baby Back

Let's read first in 1 Kings 3:16-28,

Then came there two women, that were harlots, unto the king, and stood before him.

And the one woman said, O my lord, I and this woman dwell in one house, and I was delivered of a child with her in the house.

And it came to pass the third day after that I was delivered, that this woman was delivered also; and we were together, there was no stranger with us in the house, save we two in the house.

And this woman's child died in the night; because she overlaid it.

And she arose at midnight, and took my son from beside me, while thine handmaid slept, and laid it in her bosom, and laid her dead child in my bosom.

And when I rose in the morning to give my child suck, behold, it was dead: but when I had considered it in the morning, behold, it was not my son, which I did bear.

And the other woman said, Nay; but the living is my son, and the dead is thy son. And this said, No; but the dead is thy son, and the living is my son. Thus they spake before the king.

Then said the king, The one saith, This is my son that liveth, and thy son is the dead: and the other saith, Nay; but thy son is the dead, and my son is the living.

And the king said, Bring me a sword. And they brought a sword before the king.

And the king said, Divide the living child in two, and give half to the one and half to the other.

Then spake the woman whose the living child was unto the king, for her bowels yearned upon her son, and she said, O my lord, give her the living child, and in no wise slay it. But the other said, Let it be neither mine nor thine, but divide it.

Then the king answered and said, Give her the living child, and in no wise slay it: she is the mother thereof.

And all Israel heard of the judgment which the king had judged; and they feared the king: for they saw that the wisdom of God was in him, to do judgment."

I want to draw your attention to verse 26, and write on the subject, *"Don't Get Half A Baby Back."* "Then spake the woman whose the living child was unto the king, for her bowels yearned upon her son, and she said, O my lord, give her the living child, and in no wise slay it. But the other said, Let it be neither mine nor thine, but divide it." What an amazing message in God's Word. Solomon, the king, full of the wisdom of God, is approached in his courtroom by two harlots. Newborn babies they have, one now is dead and the other is alive. At the judgment seat of Solomon they bicker back and forth. "The living child is mine. The dead child is yours," and the argument continues. Solomon, probably weary of the argument, and weary in the discussion, the fussing and feuding between them, knows exactly how to find out who the real mother of the child was. He says, "Bring a sword." Solomon takes it and raises that sword high and says, "Divide the child in half. Give half to one mother, and half to the other mother." And the real Mom cries, "O my lord, don't do this! Don't do this! Give the living child to this woman. Don't hurt my baby." Solomon says to the crying mother, "You're the real mother."

In Bible days, when a king gave the command to divide a baby in half, he meant exactly what he said. And that is exactly what would have been done. So I want to share three very serious thoughts with you.

The first thought I want to share with you is get your baby back. One mother is lying with her child next to her bosom, the other mother, rolls over on her child, and smothers her child to death. And at midnight, she sneaks up with that dead corpse in her arms, slips over to the other mother and steals the living baby, and slips that dead baby into the arms of the sleeping mother. Come morning, as they awake, one mother turns over to begin to feed the child. When she begins to feed the child, the child will not respond and will not nurse, because the child is dead. She probably screamed, wailed and travailed in her bedchamber. "My baby is dead. My baby is gone." All of a sudden, as she looked and began to examine the carcass of this dead baby, she says, "Wait a minute. This is not my baby." So she goes to the king and says, "I want my baby back. I want the living child. It is my child." She argues with the other mother in the sight of the king. And the king says, "I know exactly how to find out who the mother is." And he raises the sword over the baby. The mother cries, "Don't hurt my baby." But yet, the evil mother says,

"Go ahead, cut the baby in half. Go ahead, slash the baby in two. Don't let either one of us have a living baby." She is bitter. She is angry. She says, "I want the child cut in half," and the real mother cries and said, "O my lord, don't do this. Don't hurt my child." So the living baby is given back to the real mother. Has someone slipped in during the night, and slipped you a dead baby? Get your living baby back.

Now let's get spiritual. First of all, get your baby back. Second, don't get your baby back in half. And third, a half a baby cannot live. There is a great spiritual lesson in this for us, if we will grab it, and see it. Has the Devil come along, and taken the freshness of your relationship with Christ away? Has he taken the sweetness you had when you gave your heart to God? There is nothing sweeter than a newborn relationship. Babies are sweet, and are very precious. There is nothing sweeter, nothing more innocent than a newborn baby. And when you were born again, that is what was produced in your bosom. You became a newborn baby Christian. What a precious thing in your life! But the Devil will come to kill that baby Christian, in the night while you are asleep, in the night, while you are tarrying, in the night, while you are playing, while you are prayerless, when you are faithless, in the night, while you are wandering and piddling around in the world. The Devil slips in, tiptoes up to your bosom and slips in a dead baby. All of a sudden, you discover that you don't have the light and joy you once had. You don't even have the excitement you once had. Your baby has died.

But wait a minute. He hasn't really died. The devil just told you he died. Now are you confused again? Wait a minute, the baby is not dead, the devil just told you the baby is dead. The devil has slipped you a dead baby, while all the time, he has the living baby, and is trying to hide it from you. But when the sword of the Lord is raised high, then you see the truth, and then your excitement, and new birth cannot be taken away. You have been born again, and washed in the precious blood of Jesus Christ, and the life of Jesus still lives in your bosom.

But today, the devil tries to negotiate with you, so that you will just get back half a baby. Now think spiritually, again. Think about it. The devil wants to cripple you, so that you won't be thrilled and excited about being a born-again Christian. As a matter of fact, you don't even know if you are born again, because all you have now is half a baby. You have half the confidence, half the faith, half the excitement, half of what God has given you. You have lost it, because the devil has slipped you a lie.

I like this. There is a great spiritual truth here. Don't miss this. This is so powerful, and such a great spiritual truth that when you got saved, you received a newborn baby in your heart. The devil tries to abort it, and slips in while you are prayerless, when you've tripped or stumbled, and slips you a dead baby. So you say, "O my. I wonder if I'm saved? I wonder if God loves me anymore? Surely God won't forgive me," and you start walking under a dark cloud of condemnation and don't even know if you are saved. But I have some good news for you. That dead baby in your bosom is not your baby. It is the one the Devil slipped in on you, remember you still have a living baby, so go to the King of kings, the Lord of lords. Go to Jesus. We don't go to Solomon. We go to the wisest King of all, the King of kings, the Lord of lords, and let God raise the sword, the Bible, high and sit back and say, "Okay. God, whatever you want. I just want my baby alive."

How many pieces of babies are there? Two, three, four? That is what the devil tries to do. He tries to get you confused. Don't accept half a baby. Get your baby back. Get your confidence back. Get your excitement back. Get your walk with God back. And don't settle for half a baby, because a half a baby can't live. Half a faith can't live. Half a prayer life can't live. Half of excitement in Christ can't survive. Half of your life serving God, and the other half serving the devil can't live. And the devil knows this.

Let's make some observations about a baby. And by the way, not everyone who goes to the altar will get up changed. Not everyone who walks through the door of the church will come back again. Not everyone who gets baptized will walk in newness of life, to follow Jesus. It will only be those who will settle for nothing but the whole thing.

God gives us a little bit of heaven to keep us walking and looking toward heaven. It's true, God gives us a little bit of heaven, to go to heaven in. Have you ever gone to a Chinese restaurant? You walk into that restaurant and sit down, and the decor is different. The artwork is different. The pictures are different. The facial features of these people are different. They are from another country, and they don't look exactly like you do. Even the odor of the place is different, their ways are different, their talk is different, their music is different. And you say, "My, everything looks different around here." And that is the way God makes it when you come to church. The music is different, the talk is different, the odor is different, the ways are different, everything is different, because God wants us to be able to walk through his doors, and know that the little baby, the child or the adult who is walking in Christ can walk in church and say, "Thank God, I have some heaven to go to heaven in. Thank God there is the earnestness of the Holy Ghost in church, blessing me, helping me, and carrying me through."

When little babies are born, they are concerned only for themselves. I mean, a baby doesn't wake up at two in the morning and say, "Oh, Momma is tired. I'll just lie here a little longer and let her rest." Do you have a baby like that? No baby lies still at two or three o'clock in the morning and thinks, "Oh, isn't this so sweet? It is so quiet in here. Daddy is tired and has to go to work. Momma is tired, so I'll just not wake them until about six." No, that little baby does one thing. "Waaaaa!" Why? Nothing matters to babies except themselves. As a matter of fact, to them there is no one else in the whole world but them.

Babies, when they come into this world, are so clean, so fresh — or they can be so nasty. I take care of the fresh part, and my wife always takes care of the nasty part. Babies are so sweet, so cute, so baby powder fresh. But then, they can be so rotten. *But wait a minute. Someone has to clean up their caboose. And it isn't me. Leave me alone. Diapers, go away.*

However, babies need care. Babies must have attention. A baby can't change its own diaper. It can't feed itself. Babies have to depend upon someone bigger than them, and they are either fresh and sweet, or they stink to high heaven. Someone has to make sure they don't stink up everything. That is what I'm trying to do, to see that you are not stinking up heaven.

I told Judy, my wife, when we first got married, and she wanted to have children, "Fine. I'm making a covenant with you, right now. We'll have children, but I'll never in all my life change a diaper." I have kept that covenant through seven children. My father kept this same covenant through eleven children. The closest I ever came to breaking my covenant, (and I'm a man of my word), is when Judy was gone, and was going to be back in a few minutes, and oh my! I took one of my babies, and my goodness, I never smelled anything so bad in my entire life. I filled the bathtub with warm water and just stuck the baby, diaper and all into the bathtub. Judy came in, looked at that and said, "What are you doing?" I said, "I'm trying to survive." And I have survived, all these years. I'm the kind of guy who will get the baby powder down and sprinkle the diaper, stuff and all. However, babies need care. And if they don't get care, they are going to suffer a great deal.

When you bring a baby home, he is not considerate. He just wants what he wants, and the whole world revolves around him. Everything must be just right.

Do you remember when you first got saved? Everything had to be perfect. There couldn't be any messy sin in your life. Everything had to be exactly right. And when there was a mess, it had to be cleaned up. You cried and cried, until God cleaned you up. Isn't that right? When you first got saved, demanding as a newborn babe, and desiring the sincere milk of the word, hunger flooded your soul. You had to have God's Word. So you came to church, and hung on every word the preacher preached. And now, the preacher has to hang you on every word. There was a hunger. You were hungry for God, and forgiveness. A new born babe has been born into your bosom. You are a newborn child of God. You have been born again into the kingdom of God. Isn't it wonderful? You want attention from God. You want food from God. You need care from God, and nothing matters to you in this whole universe except the fact that you want to be perfectly right with God.

The devil says, "I'm going to slip them a dead baby;" so he begins to steal the hunger, and the desire. All of a sudden, the Devil slips in, spiritually speaking, while you are sleeping, or dabbling in the world, and playing with your gods of pleasure, and gives you a dead baby. You trip and stumble, and then you wake up the next morning and say, "Oh no, I'm not even saved. I'm not even a child of God. Now, what am I going to do?" Then you look closely, and examine a little more carefully and say, "Wait a minute. This can't be right. God is still good." Then you go to the King of kings and Lord of lords, and the sword is raised high, and Jesus says, "I'll find out if you are really a child of God. I'll divide the baby in half." And you say, "No, I don't want half a Christianity. I don't want half a prayer life. I don't want half a commitment. I don't want half a faith. I want the whole baby. Don't hurt me, God. Don't raise the sword against me. Let the baby live."

Then there will come a time in your life when the Sword will be raised high, and you will have to say, "Okay God, I'll do anything you tell me to do. Just don't hurt the baby," and judgment will come to your dwelling, when you are prayerless, when you feel like you are dead. You will come to God and say, "God, I want what I used to have. I want the walk I used to have." And God will say, "All right," and he'll raise the sword high. "Just let me divide the baby," and you will say, "No, don't do that. Let the baby live." And God will reply, "I just wanted to see if you really wanted to go on with me, if you really wanted a whole Christianity, if you wanted an all born again experience, and if you really wanted to be sold out to me." Then again, there will come a time when God will raise the Bible high. He will present you a truth, and you will have to say, "Yes, I'll step back and suffer. I'll do anything God says."

Today there are too many people who settle for half a baby, half a prayer life, half repentance toward God, half a faith, half a service to God, half a baby. And the only problem with this is, if you come to get your baby back, then don't settle for half a baby, because half a baby can't live.

You need your hunger back. Not half a hunger, all the hunger. You have to have it all back. Not half attention from God, but all attention from God.

The second thing about a baby is, a baby is totally dependent upon someone else, and in our case as Christians, we have total dependence on God. Everything is depending on God. Hebrews 11:6 says, "But without faith it is impossible to please him: for he that cometh to God must believe that he is, and that he is a rewarder of them that diligently seek him." And if you half seek him, or half believe him, or half turn to him, all you are going to get is half a baby. Don't settle for half a baby. Go to God and cry, "God, I want my baby back. I want my hunger back. I want total dependence on God once again.

John 15:5 says, "For without me ye can do nothing." But wait a minute. Do we need total dependence on God before we sing, singers? Wait a minute. Do we need total dependence on God before we go out into the world to share Christ? Do we need total dependence on God in everything we do? Yes, we do. And Jesus said, "... without me ye can do nothing." And if you are trying to do the work of God, partly in Spirit and partly in the flesh, all you have is half a baby, and it can't live. It will die. The baby will die if all you have is a half.

Last of all, a baby is innocent. That newborn baby in you is innocent. When that baby gets in trouble, it needs its innocence restored. Do you know what that is called? It is called forgiveness. And some people settle for just half a forgiveness. They settle for just half a repentance, or settle for half a response from God. Don't come to God halfway. Come to God all the way. As you approach the altar, and the throne room, do you know what is going to happen? Do you know what is going to happen to you as you approach the mercy seat, and the presence of Jesus comes? He will restore you, and make you right with God. The King of kings, and the Lord of lords, Jesus Christ, will raise the Sword high, and he will ask, "Half?" And you will have to say, "Please, don't hurt the baby. Please forgive me. If I have to suffer as a mother and walk away from my own baby, at least my baby is alive," and Jesus, out of mercy and proper judgment, will restore to you the baby.

In every decision you make, the Sword will be raised and you will be given the choice to either go the Bible way or the easy way. Are you going to go the Bible way or the carnal way, the Bible way or the way of the flesh? Are you going to go God's way, or your way? What is amazing is that the mother said, "O my lord, please, don't hurt my baby. Please, don't cut my baby in half. Just give the baby to the other woman." And the other woman said, "Cut the baby in two." But the real Momma was willing to say, when the sword was raised high, "I'll walk away, and I'll suffer. I'll suffer in the flesh. I'll give up. I'll sacrifice, just keep my baby alive." And in so doing, she got her baby back. It is the same way with you. When God raises the Sword high, and there you have to decide to obey God's Word, it may be a sacrifice. You will have to say, "I will go this way even though it's hard for me. I don't know what I am going to do. But I am willing to sacrifice. I'm willing to hurt. I'm willing to lose some things, to obey the Word of God." And when you do this, guess what? *You will get your baby back, all of him.*

Run, Chicken, Run

Now, I must confess that the headline above has little to do with this book, but you must admit, it did get your attention. Often there are those who try to run from Christian material. However, you will find this is a very interesting book. In this book, you will be encouraged and cheered up. If you don't want to be blessed, then drop this book, and run. But if you're not afraid of God's blessings, read on.

The story is told of the man who went to the bank to cash his check. After receiving his money, he stood at the window, and counted, and recounted, and recounted. The teller finally said, "What's wrong? Didn't I give you enough?" He answered, "Just barely." Life is sometimes tough, and we just have to do our best. However, it is possible to experience a great big, and wonderful God. The trouble with a lot of people is their God is too small. Apostle Paul said, "But my God shall supply all your need." Philippians 4:19. In that statement, he reveals that his God is a big God, but when you say, "My God" what do you mean? For St. Paul, "My God" meant one great enough to protect his entire life. *"My God shall supply all your need,"* he said. Unless your God is that big, then he is too small. As far as your individual life is concerned, I think God's size can be summed up in three statements:

First: God never will let you down. The psalmist had a big God. "The Lord is my shepherd; I shall not want," Psalm 23:1. That means nothing can or will happen to you that God is not able to handle. Observe those who come to Jesus in need. Not one person could ever say, "Jesus let me down." On the other hand, one after another could say, "Jesus lifted me up." *When my God becomes bigger than my needs, it means the dread and fear of my life is taken away. That doesn't mean that no trouble will ever come my way. It does mean that God will supply the strength, and the resources we need to face that trouble. God will never let us down!*

Second, God never lets you off the hook. When God created this universe, he made the laws by which it operates. It has been a long time since the creation, but earth still revolves around the sun, and the law of gravitation has not yet been repealed. Likewise, God placed into this world the principles of life. Love is better than hate; holiness is better than sin; goodness is better than evil. But as we go along, we decide we don't want to be controlled by the laws of God. So, instead of living up to God, we reduce God to the level of our living. Then, we end up with a removed God who is too little to be the Lord of our lives. So, when we decide we don't need an old-fashioned God, most of our moral convictions are eliminated. Instead of bothering about his will and his commands, we push him aside, make our own laws, and choose our own ways. In reference to God the Father, many people are lifetime teenagers. Their God is not allowed to be big enough to satisfy their lives, so they cast him aside. But remember, Jesus said that God is a father. A true father is one who keeps control over his children as long as they are children. The child may disobey, but the true father is motivated to punish that disobedience. God is a true father. We are his children, and God never lets us off the hook. Now let me say, God never lets us go.

A true picture of God is the one Jesus gave in the story of the prodigal son. When that boy wanted to leave home, and get away from the commands of his father, he was free to go. As life went on for him, that boy had some blows in the face, too! But his father didn't strike them. Life itself can be mighty cruel, hard, and disappointing. Neither did the father chase after his boy, and force him to return. Instead, the father maintained the home, and one day that boy became cold, and hungry. Then he remembered his father, and came back. The father was there with the door wide open, abundantly able to satisfy those hungers. We sometimes talk about the "free will" God has given us, as if he has completely turned us loose from himself. We are not so free. We do not have free will when it comes to eating, or not eating. Our very existence demands that we eat. And God built into us certain other hungers. It is possible to live away from God, and only hunger for material things. But there comes a time when those material things do not satisfy. We have deeper soul hungers, and those hungers are chains by which God has bound our soul. The hungers of our soul keep us dissatisfied. We seek this and that, and run here and there. But nothing we find in life satisfies our deepest needs.

Finally, we must turn to Jesus who said, *"I am the bread of life: he that cometh to me shall never hunger,"* John 6:35.

Someone has said, "Unless there is within us that which is above us, we shall soon succumb to that which is about us!" How true. Let's read again the words of Jesus Christ found in John 6:47-51,

> **Verily, verily, I say unto you, he that believeth on me hath everlasting life.**
>
> **I am that bread of life.**
>
> **Your fathers did eat manna in the wilderness, and are dead.**
>
> **This is the bread which cometh down from heaven, that a man may eat thereof, and not die.**
>
> **I am the living bread which came down from heaven: if any man eat of this bread, he shall live for ever: and the bread that I will give is my flesh, which I will give for the life of the world.**

My friend, Jesus Christ, God in flesh, was crucified on the cross for you, and then raised again from the dead. Today, he wants to be your Lord and Savior. God's power to change your life is available, and the Spirit of God awaits your prayer. The message is clear, "The wages of sin is death; but the gift of God is eternal life through Jesus Christ our Lord." Romans 6:23. You have read my sermon. Now, let me urge you to decide this matter now, once and forever.

Are you going to Heaven or Hell? Are you going to be on the side of God or Satan? It is foolish and wicked to postpone the matter. If you have not personally trusted Christ, and do not know your sins are forgiven, then I beg you, turn your heart from sin to Jesus Christ today. Admit to him that you are a sinner. Ask him to forgive you. Trust him, and commit yourself to Him to be His forever.

Put on a Happy Face

When I'm traveling, I tell Christians everywhere to confess that they are rich, good looking, and saved. That's better than being poor, lost, and ugly any day. Some say to me, "Well, two out of three isn't bad, at least I'm good looking and saved." Some even say, "one out three isn't bad, at least I'm saved." But remember, my Christian friend, when you're saved you are rich with all spiritual blessings. Also, you are good looking in Jesus Christ.

Did you ever wonder what Jesus really looked like? Seems like no two pictures we see look alike. There is good reason for this, nobody knows what he looks like. All the pictures that we see are only what someone thinks He looked like. All the Bible says about him is, *"His face did shine as the sun."* That's all. Did you ever think about how you look? Here is the way one person thought of himself. "As a beauty I'm no shining star, there are others more handsome by far. My face I don't mind it, because I'm behind it. It's the folks out in front that I jar."

Once when a young boy came down to breakfast, his father said, "You don't own your face." The young boy thought, "What's with dad?" But his father really was right. The boy had a sad countenance because he was down. But the way he looked made other family members feel way down, too.

Sometimes we say more by the look on our face than we do with words. *I wonder what Christ looked like when he took those little kids on his knee, or when he talked to the woman at Jacob's well, or when he healed the sick, or when he preached to Nicodemus, or to Mary and Martha, or when he cried, "Father, forgive them for they know not what they do."* I wonder what he looks like right now as he looks at us? As we wonder, may we see how we look.

Let me ask you a serious question: "Are you really happy?" Of course all of us have mood swings, but are you happy deep down? Someone has said, "You should do something everyday to make other people happy, even if it's only to leave them alone." Someone else has said, "I didn't know what happiness was until I got married, but then it was too late." Again, "The one who smiles when things go wrong is just going off shift."

Of course, the hard facts are, not one of us can escape ourselves. None of us can just run away. We are stuck with ourselves, but the good news is we can experience joy and happiness down deep in our hearts. First, there is the joy of having our sins forgiven, through the blood sacrifice of Jesus Christ. You see, Jesus died for our sins, paid our sin debt with his shed blood, and arose again from the dead to conquer the power of death forever. Look at these great verses in Romans 5:8-11.

But God commendeth his love toward us, in that, while we were yet sinners, Christ died for us.

Much more then, being now justified by his blood, we shall be saved from wrath through him.

For if, when we were enemies, we were reconciled to God by the death of his Son, much more, being reconciled, we shall be saved by his life.

And not only so, but we also joy in God through our Lord Jesus Christ, by whom we have now received the atonement.

My dear reader, if you would right now call upon the Lord Jesus Christ, with all your heart, something wonderful will happen to you. Getting forgiven of your sins is the most joyful thing you will ever experience.

Second, there is the joy of God's Spirit. Look at Romans 14:17, "For the kingdom of God is not meat and drink; but righteousness, and peace, and joy in the Holy Ghost."

Third, there is the joy of believing. Romans 15:13 says, "Now the God of hope fill you with all joy and peace in believing that ye may abound in hope, through the power of the Holy Ghost."

The greatest thing you can ever experience is a power greater than all the world. And the power I speak of is God's power, only by giving your life to Jesus Christ, can you find true peace and joy.

Have I Got a Story For You

A Meditation from Mark 10:46-52

Just outside the Jericho Road,
Blind Bartimaeus was begging, we're told.
Without his sight, in darkness he stumbled,
And in his heart sweet dreams had all crumbled.
The facts were sad, and his heart was blue,
But my, what a story I've got for you.
The darkness within could not keep him bound,
For from Heaven there came a brand new sound.
For in his ears the cheering was clear,
The master is near, now be of good cheer.
As Jesus came close and stood by his side,
He knew that the darkness couldn't even hide.
Then Jesus asked with his majestic voice,
What would you have me to do?
Then Blind Bartimaeus cried,
This is my choice,
My eyes, please make them brand new.
Then suddenly a thousand sensations flooded his heart,
As in the light his eyes did dart.
Hey heart! His eyes did shout,
Out of the darkness we've come out.

In his mind came this wondrous thought,
As the light of God did heal his heart.
Today, I've got a brand new start.
Now this story's not quite over,
May I talk to you?
For in your heart you may need a new start,
Your heart may be hurting, too.
At first the story is bitter,
But God will deliver.
Now listen, these stories are true,
For all have sinned and come short of God's glory,
So today let me help you,
Because you've sinned — Death and Hell must be,
But wait! God died for you, on Calvary's tree.
Christ's blood was shed upon the cross,
So you and I would suffer no loss.
Yes, you and I should die, and that's no lie,
And from Heaven God did cry.
He gave us His son, His only begotten one
For you and I, He died.
It's a fact, Christ took our place,
So He could save us by his Grace.
If in your heart it's dark and stormy,
Bow your head now, and pray for God's mercy and glory.
You need no darkness and despair of heart,
For Jesus Christ can give you a brand new start.
As I close, let me be perfectly straight,
If you die in sin, it will be too late.
So turn your heart away from sin,
And let Jesus Christ today come in.

Trust in his blood for forgiveness of sin,
And with God's Spirit a new life will begin.
Up from the grave Jesus Christ did arise,
For justification, completely surrender before God's eyes.
As I end this simple little story,
If you don't repent of sin, you'll see no glory.
If from sin, you don't let go,
Into Hell's fire, you'll forever go.
But oh what joys can flood your soul,
If from your heart you let sin go
On the Lord Jesus Christ believe with your heart,
And all of Heaven for you will start.

Chill Out, Life is Good!

My uncle John Doss told me an old joke he heard years ago about how one snowy Sunday morning a farmer went to church. When he entered, he saw that he and the preacher were the only ones present. The preacher asked the farmer if he wanted him to go ahead and preach. The farmer said, "I'm not too smart, but if I went to feed my cattle, and only one showed up, I'd feed him." So the minister began his sermon.

> One hour passed, then two hours, then three hours. The preacher finally finished, and came down to ask the farmer how he had liked the preaching. The farmer answered slowly, "Well, I'm not very smart, but if I went to feed my cattle, and only one showed up, I sure wouldn't feed him the whole truck load of hay!"**

As I write, I must confess I feel like the mosquito which landed on a very fat man. I know what to do, I just don't know where to begin.

We all know life's not perfect, but it sure is wonderful!

So let's start by saying life is not without trouble. Have you noticed, no matter how hard we wish for perfection, it just doesn't happen. Let's remember first — it won't always be perfect at work. You will have those gloomy days.

> A friend of mine told a story of a carpet layer who had worked all day installing wall-to-wall carpeting. When he noticed a lump under the carpet in

> the middle of the living room, he felt his shirt pocket for his cigarettes — Oh, Oh, they were gone! He was not about to take up the carpet, so he went outside for a two-by-four. Tamping down the cigarettes with it would be easy. Once the lump was smoothed, the man gathered up his tools, and carried them to the truck. Then two things happened simultaneously. He saw his cigarettes on the seat of the truck, and over his shoulder he heard the voice of the woman to whom the carpet belonged. "Have you seen anything of my parakeet?" Oops, another reason to quit smoking.**

Also — Religion isn't Perfect

> I remember a story where a Quaker became angry with his milk cow for kicking over a pail of milk. He warned, "Thou knowest that because of my religion, I can't punish thee. But if thou doeth that again, I will sell thee to the Baptist preacher, and he will kick thee so thee won't be able to kick it over again!"**

Now look, you may not even be religious, and that's okay, but let me at least encourage you to give God a chance. Life is not perfect, but Jesus Christ is. Look at these wonderful words from God's Word to you in John 3:16, "For God so loved the world, that he gave his only begotten son, that whosoever believeth in him should not perish, but have everlasting life." Romans 6:23, "For the wages of sin is death; but the gift of God is eternal life through Jesus Christ our Lord."

God loves you more than the devil hates you. (And we all know that the Devil has a whole lot of hate.) But God and his love are much, much bigger than all the hate of this world.

Look at the wonderful verse recorded in God's word in John 3:16. You know I have read and heard this verse many times, and it still takes my breath, just to know that the God of Heaven loves me.

Someone has said, "John 3:16 is the heartbeat of the Bible." Others say, "It is the TNT of God." Still some say, "It must be a little Bible in itself."

I personally think of an old country preacher who many years ago stood to the pulpit one Sunday morning and said, "Folks, I'm going to preach this morning on pills." He said, "Now there are white pills and yellow pills, blue pills and green pills, pink pills and black pills. There are short pills, long pills, fat pills, horse pills, sugar pills, capsules, round pills, square pills and expensive pills, but there ain't no pill like the Gos-pill." I agree!

Have you noticed John 3:16 begins with God and ends with everlasting life, and we are found in between? That means that all of us "whosoevers" can live forever. Someone has well said, "Love wasn't put in your heart to stay, love isn't love until you give it away." It also tells us God **so loved** us that he gave to us his son, Jesus Christ. The Bible tells us in Romans 6:23, "the wages of sin is death." Look, this verse puts us all in a bad position because we have all sinned. Thank God, Jesus took all of our punishment, and whosoever of us who will repent of our sins and believe on Jesus Christ will receive everlasting life.

Look, you don't need a doctorate in theology, a commentary, or a dictionary to understand that God "so" loved you that he made a way for you to live forever.

Now, let's look at this. The Bible tells in First Timothy 6:12 that we are to lay hold of eternal life. "Fight the good fight of faith, lay hold on eternal life, whereunto thou art also called, and hast professed a good profession before many witnesses.

I remember a story I heard many years ago about a couple who had a small son. This couple claimed to be atheists. When the little boy was about 12 years old, he got very sick, and was dying. The mother and father stood around the bedside and said, "Son, the doctor said you are going to die." With that the child began to cry. The father said to his agonizing son, "Hold on son, it will be over in just a little while, just hold on. The pain will cease, and you'll just go to sleep. There is nothing to be afraid of son, just hold on, just hold on. It will be over in just a little while." With that, the little guy with his face white and his eyes filled with fear and pain said, "Momma, Daddy, you're telling me to hold on, but there's nothing to hold on to."

Well, thank God, we have someone to hold on to. Jesus said, "Let not your heart be troubled. If you believe in God, believe also in me for in my Father's house are many mansions. If it were not so I would have told you. I go to prepare a place for you, and if I go, I will come again and receive you unto myself that where I am, there ye may be also."

What does it mean to lay hold of eternal life? It means lay hold of Jesus Christ. Tell him you need a new life. Tell him you are sorry about your sin. Tell him you need forgiveness. Ask him to come into your life, and he will. After all, John 3:16 is God's loving hug to all of us.

That's what you need, a great big hug from God.

Why don't you, right now, open your heart to God, and invite Jesus Christ into your life? Life is not perfect, but it can be wonderful. You may be saying to yourself, "Church just isn't my thing." I sure hope sin isn't your thing. **Give God a chance. He loves YOU!**

Come On — Sweeten Up!

Children are so wonderful. I remember just this summer, it was HOT, HOT, HOT. Because of this, my five and seven year old girls were in our swimming pool every chance they had. One evening, I came home late from a hard day's work at church. This night, I found myself standing beside the pool, where my children were swimming. Without warning to my little girls, I jumped in, dress clothes and all. Charity, who is my seven year old, along with Ju Ju, my five year old, totally flipped out. They thought that ole dad had lost it, and on top of it all, they thought I was drowning. For a moment, I thought I was, too. Well, after my girls got their little heartbeats slowed down, Ju Ju, my five year old said, "Dad, what are you doing? Pastors are not supposed to act like that."

One Sunday afternoon I took my children to Table Rock Lake to do some fishing. Judy, my five-year-old, caught what she thought to be a prize catch, and I admit, it was a pretty big perch. I said, "Honey, now let's let it go." But she insisted that she should keep it for at least a little while. She held that poor thing like you would hold a pet. Finally, she agreed to let it go. So she began her good-bye speech. She said, "Good bye, old friend," and dropped him belly up into the water. The poor fish finally wiggled a little bit, then darted down under the deep water. I thought, "Good bye, old friend! With friends like that, who needs enemies?"

On this same weekend, my mother-in-law's car had broken down. So we let her drive one of our cars. Well, Ju Ju, my five-year-old fisher girl said, "Daddy, where is Granny going with our car?" I explained that she needed to get home. Then she said, "Why don't you let her walk? She has legs, and that's what legs are for!" Now, let's not jump to conclusions. Ju Ju loves her Granny, she wasn't being sarcastic or rude, it's just that walking is not a horrible thing to her, but then she's not 76 years old, either.

My, isn't the sweet simplicity of a child wonderful? Here are some letters to God by some children.

> *Dear God,* Instead of letting people die and having to make new ones, why don't you just keep the ones you have?*
>
> *Dear God,* Maybe Cain and Abel wouldn't kill each other so much if they had their own rooms. It works with my brother and I.*
>
> *Dear God,* I bet it's hard for you to love all of everybody in the whole world. There's just four people in our family, and I could never do it.*
>
> Then there is the four-year-old girl who was returning home from the funeral service of her grandmother. Riding in the car with her was her other grandmother. "Where did Grandma go?" she asked. "We believe she went to be with God," the other grandmother replied. "How old was she?" "She was 75 years old." "How old are you?" "I am 80." The little girl thought a bit, then said, "I hope God hasn't forgotten you!"*
>
> One day a preacher was waxing eloquent as he envisioned the day of judgment. "Lightning will flash, thunder will boom, rivers will overflow ... fire

will flame from the heavens ... the earth will quake violently ... darkness will fall upon the entire earth!" Then a small boy's voice lifted from the congregation as he questioned his father, "Dad, do you think they will let school out early that day?"*

Do you know there is a lot we can learn from a child? Here is what Jesus said about the little children.

At the same time came the disciples unto Jesus, saying, Who is the greatest in the kingdom of heaven?

And Jesus called a little child unto him, and set him in the midst of them,

And said, Verily I say unto you, Except ye be converted, and become as little children, ye shall not enter into the kingdom of heaven.

Whosoever therefore shall humble himself as this little child, the same is greatest in the kingdom of heaven.

Matthew 18:1-4

Did you notice Jesus said, "Adults need to be converted?" We adults must confess something that happens to us as we suffer the hard knocks of life. We simply lose our sweetness.

There are many things we could learn from a child. I would like to suggest just a few.

First: Children depend on their parents for safety, and those of us who are grown must depend on God for our safety.

Second: The little child depends on his parents for direction, so likewise, every adult must look to the Heavenly Father for reconciliation, and guidance if they expect to be happy, and someday go to Heaven.

Third: Little children look to their parents for support. Listen, my friend, our lives can get so cluttered up. As we journey through this life, the joys we once knew as a child often vanish away. Have you noticed little children are filled with simplicity? They believe in life, and if given the opportunity, they all will sing with a faith-filled heart: *Jesus loves me! this I know, For the Bible tell me so; ... Yes, Jesus loves me; Yes, Jesus loves me! Yes, Jesus loves me! The Bible tells me so.* They have no pride to keep them from God. They have no hate to darken their little minds.

> **Brethren, be not children in understanding; howbeit in malice be ye children, but in understanding be men.**
>
> **1 Corinthians 14:20**

When I think of a child, I think of sweetness, trust, and how in their helplessness they're not afraid, or too proud to depend on their mommy and daddy. My friend, you, too, ought to join the choir of the little hearts singing: *Jesus loves me! This I know, for the Bible tells me so.*

Just think of tiny children's willingness to love, and trust. Think of the excitement in them. How they can enjoy the little things of life! Have you noticed they can have fun wherever they are? Do you remember when you laughed in childhood, but now you cannot remember why? Look, now is the time for the best laughter.

The words of a great song written by Johnson Oatman, Jr. go like this: *Count your many blessings, name them one by one. Count your many blessings, see what God hath done.* Something happened to us when we left the nursery. Sin and guilt began to fill and control our hearts so that we needed a conversion. The Bible calls it being born again. "...Repentance toward God, and faith toward our Lord Jesus Christ," Acts 20:21.

My friend, wouldn't you like to get all the sin washed out of your heart? Without the forgiveness of God, you cannot go to Heaven. "For the wages of sin is death," Romans 6:23. If you are without Jesus Christ, the judgment of God awaits you. Here is a description of this judgment from God's Word found in Revelation 20:11-15.

> **And I saw a great white throne, and him that sat on it, from whose face the earth and the heaven fled away; and there was found no place for them.**
>
> **And I saw the dead, small and great, stand before God; and the books were opened: and another book was opened, which is the book of life: and the dead were judged out of those things which were written in the books, according to their works.**
>
> **And the sea gave up the dead which were in it; and death and hell delivered up the dead which were in them: and they were judged every man according to their works.**
>
> **And death and hell were cast into the lake of fire. This is the second death.**
>
> **And whosoever was not found written in the book of life was cast into the lake of fire.**

But wait! Here is the good news. "The gift of God is eternal life through Jesus Christ our Lord," Romans 6:23.

There is no need for you to die the second death, God made it possible for you to go to heaven. *"For God so loved the world, that he gave his only begotten Son, that whosoever believeth in Him should not perish, but have everlasting life."* John 3:16. Why don't you find a place of prayer today, and ask Jesus Christ to forgive and save you from all your sins. Like a little child, trust God. Love, and believe on the Lord Jesus Christ.

Why not this Sunday load up the children in the car, and go to church. If you have no children, remember, there's another child God wants to meet, and that child is you.

Cheer Up! Cheer Up! Cheer Up!

Wouldn't it be wonderful if you could take all the bad things of your past, and make them disappear? All of us know that the past can follow us around like a long, cold, dreary day. Don't forget — the lightning bug is a bright little fellow though he doesn't have a mind, for he goes through life with his headlights on behind. It's sad, but for many, looking back is a tormenting experience, and for some reason they just keep looking back. However, Jesus Christ tells us we can find sweet peace with God despite our troubled past. In the Bible, we are promised the good cheer of forgiveness. Of course, this forgiveness is only ours through a personal encounter with Christ. Charles Spurgeon testified, when he first got saved: "I thought I could have leaped from earth to Heaven with one spring when I first saw my sins drowned in the Redeemer's blood."

In Matthew 9:2, Jesus announced to a very defeated, and sick man, "Son, be of good cheer, thy sins be forgiven thee." Forgiveness will create a very happy person, especially when our Holy God is the one doing the forgiving. But it is altogether something terrifying to pretend you're forgiven. I find myself puzzled at the way some, even good people, just pretend to be forgiven of their sins. I'm reminded of the little boy after a rain storm who, while splashing in the puddles, found a big frog. The little fellow didn't know that his pastor had been invited to his house for dinner. The little boy came running into his house with his frog, and with an excited voice said, "Look Mom, I found this frog, and I took him by his legs, and I whacked him against a tree, and I whacked him against the ground, and I whacked him against the road." Then all of a sudden the little boy looked up, and saw his pastor. His little eyes got as big as silver dollars, and he began to stutter, *"And uh, and uh, and the L-o-o-r-d called him home."*

This story reminds me of a lot of people. Down deep they know if they are really okay, or not. Listen, only true repentance toward God, and faith in the blood of Jesus Christ will create in us the good cheer of forgiveness.

Now here is another promise of joy. It's called the good cheer of no fear. In Matthew 14:27, Jesus comes walking on top of the water to his disciples. At that very same time, a very hideous storm has fallen upon them, and they are trapped in their little ship. They are absolutely terrified. Fear has overcome them. Then, like a rainbow after a storm, come the beautiful words of Jesus Christ to his disciples, "Be of good cheer. It is I, be not afraid." An old country preacher said, "Doubts and fears are like the toothache, nothing more painful, but never fatal." *Don't forget, Jesus always has the last word. So no matter what is going on in your life, remember — the good word is, "Be of good cheer. It is I, be not afraid."* Staying close to Jesus will create a very peaceful heart, and peace will produce a lot of joy.

Now here is another cheerful thought. It is called the good cheer of victory. It is found in John 16:33, "In the world ye shall have tribulation; but be of good cheer, I have overcome the world." Once again, these are the words of the perfect Son of God. This is the promise of victory. I like victory, and you do, too. There is nothing like winning. We all like to feel good about ourselves, even in the little things. I've often said, "If I were a chicken, I would want to lay the biggest egg. If I were a little bird, I would like to fly the highest. If I were a tiny dog, I would like to bark the loudest. If I were a toad frog, I would like to jump the highest. If I were a kitten, I would want to meow the sweetest. Even if I were a bad dog, I would want to bite everybody in town. And if I were a skunk, I would want to be the biggest stinker around." The sad truth is we will not always feel good about ourselves.

But we can feel good about our God. In the world we will have tribulation, *but our God is a "cheer up" God.* He knows we are going to have hard times, but if we will just stay close to him, there will be joy unspeakable. Listen, in the world you shall have tribulation — the devil is real! Don't be like the boxer who, after the first round, went back to his corner, and his trainer patted him on the back and said, "Go back, and get him this next round. He hasn't laid a glove on you." He went back, and fought the second round, and his opponent almost knocked him out. He staggered back to the corner. His trainer patted him on the back again and said, "Go back, and get him this time. He hasn't laid a hand on you!" Then he went out the third round, he was knocked down twice for the count of nine, and was saved by the bell. They dragged him back to the corner. His trainer patted him on the back and said, "Go back, and get him this next round. He hasn't laid a glove on you." He said to his trainer, "I'm going back to get him this next round, but you need to keep your eyes on that referee.

Somebody is beating the devil out of me!" Make no mistake, the devil is real, and you may not see him, but he is doing everything he can to make you miserable. So, why don't you let God cheer you up? Remember, you can always feel good about God. He will forgive you, He will be with you, and in the end, you will win.

Don't be a Hot Head

Up north there grows a tree which is the wonder of the plant world. It is only seven feet in height when it is full grown. When night comes it draws its leaves together, and curls its twigs into shapes like coils. If touched after it has settled itself for its "night's sleep," it will flutter as if agitated with the disturbance. The more often it is molested, the more vigorously the branches will shake. Finally, if the shaking continues, the tree gives off a sickening odor sufficient to inflict a headache on the disturber. This freak of nature is nicknamed the "Angry Tree."

Have you noticed in this busy world of ours that there are a host of angry people who don't need much of a shaking to make them throw off words of anger, and disgusted glances? Today there are way too many people with very low boiling points. They get ruffled quickly, and show their impatience.

> On a busy city street a car stalled in the heavy traffic as the light turned green. All the driver's efforts to start the engine failed, and a chorus of honking behind him made matters worse. He finally got out of his car, walked back to the first driver, and said, "I'm sorry, but I can't seem to get my car started. If you'll go up there and give it a try, I'll stay here and blow your horn for you."*

One day as a young mother and her very young son were driving down the street, the inquisitive little boy asked a revealing question. He asked, "Momma, why do the idiots only come out when Daddy drives?"

> There was a woman who went to a post office to buy stamps during the noon rush. This particular post office was not known for the kindness of its clerks. The stamp was pushed across the counter with such force that it landed on the floor about three feet from the counter. The woman calmly picked up the stamp, and placed the money for the stamp on the floor in place of the stamp.*

Let's look and see what the Bible says about anger. The truth is a man easily given to anger, even though he may be a Christian, is simply not right with God. Look at these three verses. "Be not hasty in thy spirit to be angry. For anger resteth in the bosom of fools," Ecclesiastes 7:9.

> **He that is slow to anger is better than the mighty, and he that ruleth his spirit than he that taketh a city.**
>
> **Proverbs 16:32**

> **The discretion of a man deferreth his anger, and it is his glory to pass over a transgression.**
>
> **Proverbs 19:11**

As I conclude, let me ask, "Why are there so many frustrated people in the world today?" Well, I'm sure you could share with me a million and one external reasons. However, the truth is the problem is on the inside of man. It is his broken and troubled heart. Jesus says to all,

> **Come unto me, all ye that labour and are heavy laden, and I will give you rest.**

Take my yoke upon you, and learn of me, for I am meek and lowly in heart, and ye shall find rest unto your souls.

Matthew 11:28,29

Once a man gives his life completely over to the Lord Jesus Christ, he can start to really live in peace. Notice these great scriptures in the Bible.

Rejoice in the Lord always, and again I say, Rejoice.

Let your moderation be known unto all men. The Lord is at hand.

Be careful for nothing; but in everything, by prayer and supplication with thanksgiving let your request be made known unto God.

And the peace of God, which passeth all understanding, shall keep your hearts and minds through Christ Jesus.

Philippians 4:4-7

So, why not put your troubled life in God's hands today?

For whosoever shall call upon the name of the Lord shall be saved.

Romans 10:13

Is There a Snake in the House?

When I was a little boy, I enjoyed throwing rocks. I threw rocks at everything. One day, my brother, Tim and I were playing king on the mountain. King on the mountain is a game in which one person picks a high spot to stand on, and the other ones does everything they can to dethrone the king. While the so-called king shouts, "I'm the king! I'm the king!"

Well, Tim selected a high spot on the roof of the outhouse. For those of you who don't know what an outhouse is, it's an outdoor toilet. So here's my brother, on top of the outhouse bragging "I'm the king of the mountain." I ordered him to jump. He replied, "No, I will not!" I said, "You better jump off of there, or I will knock you off with a rock." "I can't jump off. I'm too scared," he answered in a trembling voice. I proceeded to do what every good American boy would do. I started throwing rocks. After a few rocks whizzed past Tim's ears, off the outhouse he jumped, only to hit bottom with an injured foot. Boy, were mom and dad mad.

So what am I trying to say? Things haven't really changed now that I'm older. People still play king on the mountain, and if they don't want rocks thrown at them, they need to stop playing big shot. Most of our big cheese desires are just white washed outhouses in disguise. I've found for the most part, that the upper crust is where a few crumbs get together on the top. As for my throwing rocks, I was a bad boy and bad boys get punished by good dads.

Once a preacher friend of mine told me about a little boy, who very early one morning, made his way to the breakfast table. As he sat down, his mother noticed that her little boy's face was in bad need of a washing. After she inspected his hands, it was obvious he needed a bath. His mother then asked, "How in the world did you get so dirty so early in the morning?" With an innocent little boy's reply, he said, "Momma, I went to bed last night this way."

So many times if we are not very careful, our spiritual life ends up like this little fellow. Things just get the best of us simply because we don't stay daily at the feet of Jesus.

Here is what God's Word says in Second Corinthians 7:1, "Dearly beloved, let us cleanse ourselves from all filthiness of the flesh and spirit, perfecting holiness in the fear of God." Now I am by no means implying that a little boy's dirty face is sin. That would be absurd. However, there are sins of the flesh and spirit that all of us must watch out for.

> One Saturday night, as many people were preparing to turn out their lights, the lights in one community all went out by themselves. Air conditioners suddenly quit running. Houses everywhere were without power. It seemed strange that this would happen on a night when there were no storms in the area. While their homes grew warmer in the August heat, and their patience grew thinner, people wondered what had caused the power outage. The power was off most of the night, and it was the next day before they found out what had caused the problem. A whole community had lost power for most of

the night because a big black snake had gotten into the powerhouse, and messed things up.*

If we experience life that is ineffective, and without power, the problem is not that our God lacks the power. The problem may be a snake in the powerhouse. Something in our life, some disabling sin that does not belong in our life. We must be careful what we allow to crawl into our lives.

Let me recommend this prescription.

Get Jesus, and through Him get thoroughly right with God. Then get thoroughly right with your loved ones. Get out of the rat race, and enjoy a peaceful, clean life. Get in church and stay there. God often makes major adjustments while God's people worship, and the man of God preaches.

So why not, right now, *get moving* in the right direction.

Bad Habits

It's certainly no secret that a bad habit can hinder a Christian's WITNESS, as well as bring shame and guilt to one's own life.

Look, if you want to break a bad habit — drop it, it will break. Am I saying that a habit is easy to break? No! No! No! Sometimes it's almost impossible.

If you take the "H" out of habit, you've still got "a-bit." If you take the "A" off "a-bit," you still have "bit." Take the "B" off of "bit," and you still have IT. Now, what's the cure?

First, admit your habit is wrong. You will never drop it until you do.

Second, depend on God's power, not yours, to overcome.

Third, make that determined decision to drop it.

Fourth, when tempted to pick it up again, pray! pray! pray! Then, stay with your decision.

Above all, replace your used-to-be bad habit with some good habits.

Good habits? Sure! How about a habit of prayer, or a habit of studying God's Word? Or how about a stubborn habit of wanting to be free, that is so stubborn, when the Devil says: "why not?", there will be a righteous anger grip your soul, and out of your spirit will come the cry of prayer, the power of God's word, and the shout of VICTORY as you say NO! to the devil, and YES! to Christ!

Liquor Has No Defense

In all the miracles that Jesus performed, the one found in John 2 is the most misunderstood. In this chapter, we find that Jesus turned the water into wine. My, if only I had a nickel for every time I've heard this quoted by those in defense of drinking. I'd be a very rich man. However, any kind of intoxicating wine, or mild liquor is wrong. Wrong for our children, wrong for our families, wrong for our churches, wrong for our community, wrong for our cities, and wrong for our nation. Wrong, wrong, wrong!

Now, did the water that Jesus turned into wine become intoxicating? First, let's remember Jesus was the perfect man, and still is our perfect Savior, forever. Here is what the Bible says about wine and strong drink. Notice the Bible puts wine and strong drink together. Proverbs 20:1, "Wine is a mocker, strong drink is raging: and whosoever is deceived thereby is not wise."

> **Who hath woe? who hath sorrow? who hath contentions? who hath babbling? who hath wounds without cause? who hath redness of eyes?**
>
> **They that tarry long at the wine; they that go to seek mixed wine.**
>
> **Look not thou upon the wine when it is red, when it giveth his colour in the cup, when it moveth itself aright.**

At the last it biteth like a serpent, and stingeth like an adder.

Proverbs 23:29-32

No, I do not believe Jesus created intoxicating wine. I have several good reasons for this conclusion. First, Jesus would not disobey the scriptures. In the Old Testament book of Habakkuk 2:15, *"Woe unto him that giveth his neighbor drink, that puttest thy bottle to him, and makest him drunken also, that thou mayest look on their nakedness!"* Second, when God created the earth, nothing was harmful, or evil. The lion did not kill, the snake did not bite, and the adder did not sting. When Jesus turned the water into wine, I am sure he stayed in the guidelines of what was pure, and holy. If the wine that Jesus made had any power in itself, it was to make people joyful, or happy. I'm sure that this would have been its only power. Just as the rose was without a thorn in the beginning of creation, you can rest assure that the wine Jesus created was without its thorn of intoxication. Jesus always brought out the best of those he came in contact with. Both the wine and liquor often times brings out the worst in a man, not to mention, it distorts man's thinking, and his ability to function normally. I can hear the argument now, "But I don't get drunk." Have you ever gotten drunk? Proverbs 23:31 commands us not to even look upon the wine when it is red, when it gives his color in the cup, or when it moves itself aright. *In blunt talk, we are not to even look at, or desire a glass of fermented wine.*

Then there are those who say, "Well, I'm from the old country, and my forefathers drank wine because of a lack of good water." Yes, and your forefathers got drunk on occasions, too.

Now, do you really think there is more wine in the world than there is water? Are you going to put wine in a baby bottle, or a child's cup? You're forgetting, the Bible first arrived from Heaven to the Middle East. *Remember, when the children of Israel were in the wilderness, God gave them water out of a rock, not wine out of a rock.* I drink soda pop because I want to. I drink milk because I want to. I don't have to drink pop, or milk because there is no water. Don't say there is no drinking water, or juice, or milk in other far away countries. I'm not that naive. People drink intoxicating wine because they want to, not because they have to.

As much as we deplore the tragedy of war in the Far East, and the thousands of our men who have been slain there, it is shocking but true, that far more people have been killed in one year because of beer, wine, and whiskey in the United States! Alcoholism is the number three killer in America today! Alcohol shortens life. Drinking people have three times the mortality rate. Shakespeare cried, "Oh, thou invisible spirit of wine. If thou hast no name to be known by, let us call thee devil!" Abraham Lincoln said, *"Liquor has no defense."*

Can You Answer the Following Questions?

I remember when, as an evangelist, I was a guest speaker at a little country church called Union Grove. It was located just outside the small town of Aurora, Mo. This particular Sunday morning, the adults were having an open discussion in the Sunday School class. They were expressing how God created each one of us as a unique person, and no two of us are just alike. One brother said, "I thank God that everybody is not just like me. If they were just like me, everyone would want my wife." With that, this man's wife giggled and smiled. All of a sudden, from the back of the auditorium came a rough voice saying, "My brother, if everyone were just like me, no one would want your wife."

Question to All the Husbands:

Is love really blind, or is your wife a real looker?

Many years ago I heard of a story about a farmer who purchased a donkey. The man who sold him the animal warned him that the donkey would work well, provided he would show it a lot of love and affection for one week.

However, in spite of all, the donkey wouldn't budge. Disgusted, the farmer complained to the dealer that he either had to correct the problem, or return his money.

The man went to the farm and saw immediately that the donkey was very well taken care of and loved by the farmer. He then picked up a large club in the barn, and slapped the donkey over the head with it. Horrified, the farmer shouted, "I thought you said I should show him love and affection." Then replied the dealer, "Sure, but you have to get his attention first."

Question to All Stubborn People:

Do you need pampered, or hit with a club?

I heard another story about a mother visiting a department store. While there, she took her son to the toy department. Finding a gigantic rocking horse, he climbed upon it, and rocked back and forth for almost an hour. "Come on, son," the mother pleaded. "I have to get home to get daddy's dinner." The little boy refused to budge, and all her efforts were unavailing. The department manager also tried to coax the little fellow, without meeting any success. Eventually, in desperation, they called for a child psychiatrist. Gently he walked over and whispered a few words in the boy's ear, and immediately the boy jumped off and ran to his mother's side. "How did you do it?" the mother asked incredibly. "What did you say to him?" The psychiatrist hesitated for a moment, then said, "All I said was, "If you don't jump off of this rocking horse at once, boy, I'll knock the stuffing out of you!"**

Question to All Parents of Small Children:

Do you beg a child to behave, or make him?

Now, in order to keep your attention, I have a few more mind bending questions. Some I have created myself, and some I heard years ago. So here we go!

First to the preachers: If you have a funeral at night, do people drive with their lights off?

To the farmer: If a hog kills himself, is it hog-icide or sooey-cide?

To the ladies: When it rains, why don't sheep herds shrink?

To the Ecologist — The concerned environmentalist: What does an Ecologist do when one discovers an endangered animal who eats endangered plants?

To the business man: When a company ships Styrofoam, what do they pack it in?

To the dairy farmer: Why do you put an expiration date on sour cream?

To the policeman: If you have someone with a multiple personality disorder, and he threatens to kill himself, do you consider that a hostage situation?

To the social worker: If a turtle does not have a shell is it homeless or naked?

To the cook: Does a strange meat dish always taste like chicken, and if it does why not just eat the chicken?

To the kids: If you choke a Smurf, what color does he turn?

To the men: If there is a man standing all alone in a forest, and there is no woman to hear him, and he makes a statement, is it still wrong?

Okay, Here are Some More Questions, Only These are Very Serious!

First: Is there a God, and if there is, are you ready to meet him?

Here is what the inspired Word of God tells us:

And as it is appointed unto men once to die, but after this the judgment:

So Christ was once offered to bear the sins of many; and unto them that look for him shall he appear the second time without sin unto salvation.

Hebrews 9:27,28

Here's another question: If all sin has to be punished or paid for, how could any of us pay the bill?

Another question: If God so loved the world that he gave his only begotten son to pay our sin debt, shouldn't we listen to God?

Another question: If there is a real Hell, or even the smallest chance of one, wouldn't you be a real fool to reject Jesus Christ?

Another question: Isn't eternity too long for you to be wrong?

Last question: *If you have a no-God attitude, and this Jesus stuff just isn't for you, don't you think that judgment day will be the saddest day of your eternity?*

And the devil that deceived them was cast into the lake of fire and brimstone, where the beast and the false prophet are, and shall be tormented day and night for ever and ever.

And I saw a great white throne, and him that sat on it, from whose face the earth and the heaven fled away; and there was found no place for them.

And I saw the dead, small and great, stand before God; and the books were opened: and another book was opened, which is the book of life: and the dead were judged out of those things which were written in the books, according to their works.

And the sea gave up the dead which were in it; and death and hell delivered up the dead which were in them: and they were judged every man according to their works.

And death and hell were cast into the lake of fire. This is the second death.

And whosoever was not found written in the book of life was cast into the lake of fire.

Revelation 20:10-15

My friend, God made a way for you to go to Heaven. It's all up to you, what you do with God's precious son.

For the wages of sin is death; but the gift of God is eternal life through Jesus Christ our Lord.

Romans 6:23

Seek ye the Lord while he may be found, call ye upon him while he is near:

Let the wicked forsake his way, and the unrighteous man his thoughts: and let him return unto the Lord, and he will have mercy upon him; and to our God, for he will abundantly pardon.

Isaiah 55:6,7

Remember, forever is too long to be wrong! May you make peace with God through the blood of Jesus Christ.

You Better Learn to Fly

Or You are Going to Hit Mighty Hard Someday

God's desire is that we live in heavenly places — in his provision, his anointing and his presence. The only way for us to do this is to get up higher. We have to learn to fly, or we will spend our lives living a life of defeat, doubt and unbelief. We will miss the power, the freshness, the anointing, and the grace of God in our lives.

> **For the Lord's portion is his people; Jacob is the lot of his inheritance.**
>
> **He found him in a desert land, and in the waste howling wilderness; he led him about, he instructed him, he kept him as the apple of his eye.**
>
> **As an eagle stirreth up her nest, fluttereth over her young, spreadeth abroad her wings, taketh them, beareth them on her wings:**
>
> **So the Lord alone did lead him, and there was no strange god with him.**
>
> **He made him ride on the high places of the earth ...**
>
> **Deuteronomy 32:9-13**

What an amazing picture there is in these verses of God's love for his people. Verse 10 says God found his people in the desert land, in a wilderness. He led them about and instructed them, and he kept them as the apple of his eye. I'm told that in the Hebrew, the apple of his eye actually meant the pupil of his eye. It is the most sensitive part of God's eye. He keeps you in the pupil of his eye. He watches you. He takes care of you. He loves you. And he leads you. I can't begin to express to you how much God loves you.

And then, in Verse 11, God is pictured like a mother eagle, who stirs up her nest, flutters over her young, spreads her wings, and then takes her little eaglets on her back and bears them up...and she begins to fly high in the heavens. What is she doing? She is teaching her babies to fly. *And you'd better learn to fly, too, or you are going to hit mighty hard someday.* Why is it we are up and then down, up and then down? God wants you to learn to get up, and up, and up, not down. That is the whole process of the Bible, that we go up, down, up, down, until we are going up, up, up, never to descend back into defeat.

I want to share something with you about the eagles. The eagle fascinates me. What an amazing bird. As a matter of fact, God asked Job, "Did you command? Are you the one who is responsible for how the eagle flies, and bears the wind upon her wings? Are you responsible for how she makes her nest on the cleft of the rock, how she looks from the nest for her prey, and eats of the blood of the land." Of course, Job realized that there is nothing more fascinating than this big eagle, and he had nothing to do with its creation.

Solomon, who was the wisest man on earth other than Jesus, said, "There be three things which are too wonderful for me, yea, four which I know not: The way of an eagle in the air, the way of a serpent on a rock; the way of a ship in the midst of the sea; and the way of a man with a maid." The way of an eagle in the air is awe-inspiring. The eagle is a beautiful bird, and God said, "I took my people like the eagle, and I lifted them up on my wings."

The eagle's nest can get as large as an automobile. Eagles usually have two to three eaglets, and that nest will begin to fill up as the birds start to grow. That mother will feed those little eaglets, and as they take on the beauty of their mother, and they get bigger and bigger. The eagle will make her nest way up high in the mountains, way up high in the cliffs. She will find a solid and secure place. There is no way you can get to that nest. You can't climb up to it. You can't go over the top, and go down to it. There is no way you can get to that nest except by air. And if you leave the nest, you either go up or down, one way or another.

The mother eagle makes the nest out of thorns, and she takes her feathers and puts them around the thorns. As those eaglets begin to get bigger and bigger, heavier and heavier, those thorns begin to poke those little birds. They discover it is not as nice being in the nest, and they get crowded and irritated, acting like a bunch of church people I know—fussing and feuding. They begin to bite and devour one another. They don't know what to do with themselves when they get crowded.

The mother comes and flaps her wings, fluttering over the nest. She gets their attention, and gets those birds upon her back, because it is time to fly, and she will take them way up, miles high into the sky. Oh, those little birds are having a good time riding on Momma. Whee! This is good. This is wonderful. Then all of a sudden, Momma is way up, and they look down at the mountains that look like dots. All of a sudden Momma goes flip! And Baby goes down. That bird flutters, tumbles and tumbles. Just before that little eaglet is ready to crash, Momma will fly underneath it, lift it back up into the heavens and take it safely to the nest. I'm told that Momma will sometimes wait until the little bird is only three to six feet from the ground and utter disaster before she swoops down and catches her baby up. That little eaglet probably goes," Phew! Sure glad Momma caught me. I just about got it."

Here is the lesson. The whole purpose of Momma stirring the nest it to get those birds out of the nest. They are not supposed to stay in the nest all their life. Eagles are not supposed to live on the ground. Their nature is to be in the heavens. And Christians are not to live on the ground either. Their nature, the God-nature in their heart when they are born again, is to live in heavenly places. The eagle only comes down to the ground as it is pursuing its prey.

Here is Momma. She is stirring up the nest. The thorns are beginning to stick. The little eaglets are getting discontent. They don't know what to do. They are getting almost as big as Momma. Momma comes along and an eaglet says, "I want to try. It is my turn." The other one says, "You better not, it just about killed me." Here comes Momma. She gets that little bird up, she coos around that nest. The bird gets to playing, jumping up and down on her back. All of a sudden, Momma goes out, up into the heavens again. That little bird goes, "Yahoo! This is fun." All of a sudden Momma, all the way up to the highest height, flips over.

Man, I'll never get out of church. I'll never miss. I'll never quit. This is wonderful! I'm going to stay in church the rest of my life. I'm going to serve God the rest of my life. Boy, I'll tell you, I'm going to pay my tithes. I'm going to work for God. I'm going to soul win. I'm going to sing for the Lord. I'm going to preach the Gospel. I'm going to stand for Jesus until the world is on fire. Glory to God! Hallelujah!

FLIP! I quit. If this is being a Christian, I don't want it. And there you go. H-E-L-P! You hope the parachute opens, but you aren't wearing one. You are in big trouble. By the way, your Bible is like a parachute it is no good unless it is opened.

That bird is going down. The whole purpose in dropping him is to get that little fellow flying. Momma is teaching him to fly.

Like an eagle, you are either flying as you are supposed to; or you are saying, "I want to go. Let me go. I want to fly. Let me go up into the heavens. Let me fly high in the sky. Let me be with you." You are praying, "God help me. God make me a great man of God. Make me a great woman of God. Help me. I want the power of God." "Okay," God says, "Get on my back." FLIP! And you say, "No, no, not that way, God." But that is the way it happens. That is the way you get it. You have to learn to fly.

One of these days you are going to take your last flight lesson. This must be the saddest time for the mother eagle. She will coo to those babies. She will love them. She will feed and nurture those babies. She will take them up and give them flying lessons over and over and over again. She will almost let them hit the ground and then she will fly right under them. You say, "Whoa! God rescued me. Glory to

God! He is so good. I'm a great Christian." No, you are not—until you learn to fly. Momma Eagle knows when her babies get big, she has to let them go, because she needs to fill the nest again. Besides, eagles have to fly. They weren't made to walk. If they don't fly, eagles die. When Momma takes them up for the last time, she desperately wants them to fly. Lesson after lesson, she has pulled them out of the fire. Lesson after lesson, she has grabbed them before they hit the ground. Time after time she has rescued them from tragedy. When the last flying lesson comes, maybe she has a tear in her eye, as she says, "Please, baby, you have to fly. I won't catch you this time. You have to stretch your wings. You have to make it. This is the last run." That baby eagle has been given everything he needs to fly. He has been taught the secrets of the wind. He just needs to spread those great and mighty wings and soar back up. There will be no more free rides.

There are many people in church today who have taken a free ride for years, and one of these days, down they will go. And God won't be there at the bottom. You may think, "God will always rescue me. God will always be there for me." No, there is a last time. There is a last flight. Proverbs 29:1 says, "He, that being often reproved, hardeneth his neck, shall suddenly be destroyed, and that without remedy." You will cry, "Help me. Help me, God. I'm falling. God, rescue me out of this mess again, please. I don't want to stay in church, God. I don't want to stay in prayer, God. I don't want to stay in the Bible, God. I want to do what I want to do. I want to live the way I want to live. I don't want to be committed. God, I'll make you a promise, if you will rescue me one more time, if you will catch me from the death of the ground, God, I promise I'll pay my tithe. I promise I'll stay in church. I promise I'll serve you, God. I promise I'll work for you." And God will say, "I've heard that a million times. I've taken you on a thousand flying lessons. I've carried you up on my wings. I've loved you and cared for you. I've given you lesson after lesson. This is the last lesson. You are going to have to stretch your wings. You are going to have to learn to fly. Fly! You can't hit the ground. You can't backslide. You can't go back to sin. You have to fly, eagle. You have to bear your wings up. I can't carry you any longer. I'll fly with you in the heavens. I'll help you. I'll nurture you. I'll train you. I'll instruct you. But you have to learn to fly."

If the little eagle won't fly, there will be a tragedy! Sometimes a mother eagle will lose an eaglet that way. That great beautiful bird, wing spread six, ten, or twelve feet, with all the right equipment — the strength is there, the wings are there, the beauty is there yet that beautiful eagle tumbles and crashes into the bushes or treetops, or the cliffs of the rocks and hits the ground. And that bird, once a little eaglet but now a big eagle, lies splattered on the ground, destroyed because it wouldn't learn to fly.

Have you learned? Have you learned not to get out of church when you get discouraged? No? Then you haven't learned to fly. Have you learned to preach when you didn't feel like preaching? No? Then you haven't learned to fly. If you don't keep on praising God when everything around you is devastated, then you haven't learned to fly. Have you learned to pay your tithe even when you can't pay your bills? No? Then you haven't learned to fly. And one of these days, the great eagle won't catch you.

You will find yourself crushed beneath the bushes, the cliffs, the rocks, and the dust of the earth. You will find yourself grounded, never to fly in the heavens again.

Don't misunderstand me, because we will always need God, but if an eagle doesn't learn to fly, it can't survive. So what is the problem? It is the flying lessons. You see, all the time you have been saying, "Well, that Devil is really putting me through a hard time," it may have been God giving you a flying lesson. Maybe God is dropping you. "Well, I don't believe God tempts me." The Bible says God doesn't tempt man with evil. He doesn't, but God does test. If I build a great ship, what do I do with that ship once it is built? I put it in water to see if it will float. If it sinks, is it a good ship or a bad ship? The test is to float. If I build an airplane, what is the ultimate test? If it doesn't fly, then it is of no use. The ultimate goal of God for your life is for you to reign with him in heavenly places; you are meant to fly in the heavens.

Some people stay on the ground and get splattered by the hail, the wind, the rain, and the storms. They walk on the ground and get hit by the mud. Others fly in the clouds and get tossed about with the lightning, the winds, and the storms. But the best place to be is up above the clouds, looking down at the storm, saying, "It is peaceful up here. There is joy up here. There are blessings up here." When you reach the Heavenly places, that is where God wants you.

So, the flying lessons are these: You learn to fly. You start going to church. You start serving God. You pay your tithe. You do what you are supposed to do, and start turning your life to God. Don't be surprised when a storm begins to rage, when every demon in Hell seems to be coming against you, when everything seems to be going wrong. Isn't it wonderful — God is teaching you to fly!

You may have read a greater message, or heard a better sermon preached than this one, but you have never read a greater truth. *You'd better learn to fly, or you're going to hit mighty hard someday.*

Hey, God, I Know You're Up There!

The Psalmist was right when he said that the heavens declare the glory of God.

I know there cannot be a here without a there. There cannot be a before without an after. There cannot be an upper without a lower. There cannot be a creation without a creator. Recently I heard of a man who had regularly prayed for many years, and began to wonder if God heard his prayers at all. During one of his routine times of prayer, he started this doubting pattern once again. He stopped praying, and thought for a moment. "Enough of this," he said. He then lifted his eyes toward Heaven and yelled, "Hey, up there, can you hear me?" There was no response. He continued, "Hey, God, if you really hear me, tell me what you want me to do with my life." A voice from above thundered a reply, "I want you to help the needy, and give your life for the cause of peace!" Faced with more of a challenge than the man wanted, he answered, "Actually, God, I was just checking to see if you were there." The voice from above now answered with disappointment: "That's all right, I was only checking to see if you were there."

Let us never forget God answers prayer. Look at this wonderful verse found in the book of Jeremiah 33:3 God says,

Call unto me, and I will answer thee, and shew thee great and mighty things, which thou knowest not.

I heard of one little girl, trying very hard to remember this verse. Cautiously she recited, "Call unto me ..." she paused briefly, and then hurriedly finished, "and I will call you right back!"

My good friend, God would really like to hear from you. Prayer is a wonderful privilege. God bless you as you come to the Father in Jesus' Name.

Here Kitty, Kitty

I've heard the story of Daniel in the den of lions preached many times. I've heard preachers preach the sermon about Daniel being thrown into the den of lions, how God sent his angel to shut the mouths of the lions. I've heard it in Sunday School. I've heard songs sung about how God delivered Daniel from the den full of lions. I've heard it taught. I've read it in my Bible. I've seen it in children's books, and certainly Sunday School literature to young people. There is nothing more exciting than the old stories in the Bible about the miracle working power of God.

I've heard many sermons preached about this king Darius, and how he made a decree that no man could pray, and ask anything except from him, how Daniel went and prayed, just as he had prayed three times a day to his God. Someone told the king that Daniel was breaking the law, anyway his law, and because of the decree the king had made, he could not forfeit that decree, because it had been made under the laws of the Medes and Persians which would not be altered in any way. I've read how the king went and spent the night, trying to figure out how to rescue his friend, Daniel. You know the story. Come morning, after not resting all night, the king declared that Daniel was to be thrown into the den full of lions. There he was to be eaten up. But if you will remember, the king made this statement. "Thy God whom thou servest continually, he will deliver thee," Daniel 6:16. That night, he spent a restless night. Next morning he arose, and went quickly to the den, rolled away the stone, and cried in a very pitiful voice, "O Daniel, servant of the living God, is thy God, whom thou servest continually, able to deliver thee from the lions?" Daniel 6:20. And Daniel shouted with a loud voice, "O king, live for ever. My God hath sent his angel, and hath shut the lions' mouths," Daniel 6:21,22.

What an amazing story! I've heard it preached on many times, but I have never, in all my ministry, heard it preached on as a type and picture of redemption. In this book, I'm going to share with you what it is saying, and exactly what is taking place in this great miracle God had provided for Daniel. And by the way, he has provided a great miracle for us, too.

> **Then the king commanded, and they brought Daniel, and cast him into the den of lions. Now the king spake and said unto Daniel, Thy God whom thou servest continually, he will deliver thee.**
>
> **And a stone was brought, and laid upon the mouth of the den; and the king sealed it with his own signet, and with the signet of his lords; that the purpose might not be changed concerning Daniel.**
>
> **Then the king went to his palace, and passed the night fasting: neither were instruments of music brought before him: and his sleep went from him.**
>
> **Then the king arose very early in the morning, and went in haste unto the den of lions.**
>
> **And when he came to the den, he cried with a lamentable voice unto Daniel: and the king spake and said to Daniel, O Daniel, servant of the living God, is**

> **thy God, whom thou servest continually, able to deliver thee from the lions?**
>
> **Then said Daniel unto the king, O king, live for ever.**
>
> **My God hath sent his angel, and hath shut the lions' mouths, that they have not hurt me: forasmuch as before him innocency was found in me; and also before thee, O king, have I done no hurt.**
>
> **Then was the king exceeding glad for him, and commanded that they should take Daniel up out of the den. So Daniel was taken up out of the den, and no manner of hurt was found upon him, because he believed in his God.**
>
> **Daniel 6:16-23**

My text verse is verse twenty, "And when he came to the den, he cried with a lamentable (pitiful) voice unto Daniel: ...O Daniel, servant of the living God, is thy God, whom thou servest continually, able to deliver thee from the lions?" And we all know the answer. "Yes!" That's the answer. He is able. And he sent his angel to shut the mouths of the lions.

This is a beautiful picture and a type of redemption. And as Daniel wipes the sweat from his face and says, "Praise God, I made it," there is a great, wonderful truth being embedded in the hearts and lives of the church of Jesus Christ, and that is the truth of God delivering his people from the mouth of the roaring lion, the devil. What an amazing story!

I want you to grab this truth. There are *three characters* in this chapter I want us to take notice of, and then there are some creatures I want us to take notice of.

The first character is *Darius, the king*. He is the king who wanted to be God. Then there is *Daniel.* He is the servant of God, the child of God. We should want to be like him. We should desire to be like Daniel, as a child and servant of God, serving God continually. As a matter of fact, verse three of this chapter says, *an excellent spirit was in him.* And by the way, I have that same excellent spirit, and it is called the Holy Spirit. Also, I believe when it says Daniel had an excellent spirit, it wasn't just referring to the Spirit of God, but it was also referring to his commitment, dedication, and his consecration to God. I want to have that commitment. Someone said Daniel didn't bow, Daniel didn't crunch under the pressure. Someone said the reason the lions didn't eat Daniel is because he had too much backbone in him. And I believe he had concrete for a backbone. The lions didn't even touch him because of the power of God.

So there is Darius, who was the king, and wanted to be God. Then there is Daniel who was the servant of God, in which we ought to want to be like him. Then there are the accusers, who were messengers of Satan. According to Revelation 12:10, the devil is the *accuser of the brethren.* And he accuses the people of God before the throne of God, day and night. These people accused Daniel of breaking the law of the king Darius.

Then there are the creatures, which are the *lions.* In verse twenty-four, it tells us about the lions being very hungry, very fierce, very dangerous, and they certainly shed blood. In that verse twenty-four, it said that after Daniel came out of the den of lions, those who were cast in were eaten up, down to the bones, before they ever touched the bottom of the lions' den. We see the creatures as the hungry lions.

Now what an amazing decree how Daniel shows us that God truly has delivered us from the mouth of

Satan, himself, and we are victorious through the blood of Jesus Christ. I trust this will help you, and you will be able to say to the devil, "Here Kitty, Kitty, Kitty." And you can box his jaws with the Word of God.

We know the story, and some of this is going to just be rehearsal and review that you have heard in the past. Darius the king, like many people who get into authority, (if they are not careful) let pride grab their heart. The king had placed presidents and princes over his kingdom, and among those presidents and princes was Daniel. The Bible says Daniel was a man with an excellent spirit, and because of that, king Darius chose Daniel to be the president over his kingdom. Now, the president, princes, etc., their charge was to make sure that the kingdom ran smoothly, and they would give an account of what was happening in the kingdom to Darius. I think it is obvious in chapter six, that the king loved Daniel. What an amazing man was Daniel, the man of prayer, the man who wouldn't bend, the man who wouldn't bow, the man who wouldn't crunch under the lions' teeth, the man who stood for right. There he kept a great spirit of integrity around the king. This king chose him to be the top person in his kingdom, under him.

Now this made others jealous. Some of the other princes under Daniel decided, "We are going to get this guy. We are going to clobber him. We are going to accuse him. We are going to get him." So they tried to find out if he did things wrong. They would try to discover if he embezzled money, so they examined the books and found out that he was not embezzling money. It looked like he was giving money to the king. They began to look and see what he was doing. Was he being unfaithful to the king? Was he speaking negatively of the king? Oh no, he always spoke with great reverence of the king. There was a man of utmost precious integrity. And they couldn't find a blemish in him. Then they said, "If we are going to get this man, we have to get him through his God. We have to get him through the commandments of his God." And they began to watch him, and one of the first things they discovered about Daniel, not only did he have an excellent spirit, not only was he honest, pure, and upright before all the kingdom, but that he prayed three times a day with his face toward Jerusalem, worshipping and honoring his God. When they saw that he was a man of prayer, they said, "We can get him there. That is the only place we can get him. We can get him on this religious matter." So they decided they were going to talk the king into getting full of pride, so he would claim to be God himself. "Sign the decree, the Persian and Medes' decree that could not be altered, or changed." He was tricked by these other people to sign this decree, that if any man was to ask anything of a god, or any other man, that man who defied the decree, that he must go to king Darius and ask, he could not ask anyone else for anything. They said, "We can get Daniel. There is no way he is going to stop praying to his God." And they talked Darius into signing the decree, because they knew Darius could not get out of it once he signed it. And Darius got full of pride, and he was the king that wanted to be God. He decided, "I'll make everyone in my kingdom come to talk to me, to ask me, to pray to me." So he signed it, and little did he know these people were plotting to lynch, persecute, and kill Daniel, his very good friend.

So they watched Daniel. The decree was declared. The decree was signed, and it was heralded across the kingdom. The trumpets blew. No one could pray to God. They could not ask anyone for anything, except they came to king Darius.

Now they said, "It's time to get Daniel." So they tiptoed up to the windows, and caught Daniel praying. Daniel probably heard the decree. I'm sure he did. They probably said, "Daniel, have you heard, you can't pray anymore?" Daniel probably chuckled real loud and said, "That's what they think." Maybe one of the pious religious Pharisees of that day, offered his counsel to Daniel, and said, "Daniel, listen, we know you have to pray, but after all, you can pray silently from your heart, and God will still hear you. You don't have to open the window. You don't have to pray loud. Just go into your closet so they can't see you pray. You can still pray to God." And Daniel said, "I'm not going to compromise. I'm not going to bend. I'm not going to bow to pressure." And I believe Daniel went home, not to violate the law, not to entice or irritate the king, but, I believe, he went just as he always did, three times a day. *"My routine is not going to stop. My praise to God is not going to end. My dedication to the living God is not going to stop. I'm going to do what I'm supposed to do."* So, Daniel just went into his house, with the windows open, with his face toward Jerusalem, and prayed to his God. I believe he prayed aloud. I believe he prayed loud and clear. Maybe his prayer went something like this, "Now God, the little peeping toms are outside this building. Would you bless them, too? Now God, the little peepers are looking in, and listening to me pray. Would you just bless them real good?" And bless them real good he did. They ended up getting crunched by the lions themselves. Listen to me, and listen carefully. God will bless His children when they pray. God will bless His children when they won't compromise, and when you stand for truth. God will bless you.

Then, they went to Darius, and said, "Your friend, Daniel, he is praying." And maybe Darius said something like this, "So? I don't care. He's my friend. No big deal." "Wait a minute, King. It is a big deal. Hast thou not signed a decree, that every man that shall ask a petition of any God or man within thirty days, save of thee, O king, shall be cast into the den of lions?" The king answered and said, "The thing is true, according to the law of the Medes and Persians, which altereth not." "Well, yeah, I did do that." "Then you have to do it. You have to stick to your own commandment, King. You can't alter it. You have to stand beside it."

The Bible said he spent all that day trying to figure out, "How can I get around this? How can I keep from killing my friend?" And he couldn't come to any conclusion. All night he probably wept, and couldn't sleep, spending hour upon hour in agony. "Here I am, going to have to put my best friend into the den of lions." I believe he was the king's best friend. Maybe not physically, but I know he was the king's best friend, in the fact that Daniel prayed for him every day. And by the way, people who pray for you are your friend. They love you. They care for you, and you need friends who will pray for you.

Here it is. The king couldn't get out of it. So now he got up, after worrying all night, trying to find a way to get out of it. He had himself in trouble. Any time you decide you want to take God's place, you are going to back yourself into a corner you can't get out of. Any time you start playing with something that is God's business, you are going to get it so entangled, you are never going to get it straightened out. Any time you stick your nose where it doesn't belong, concerning spiritual and godly matters, you are going to get into a mess. You are going to get into trouble. You are going to get into a place where you can't get out, because you are not God. Step aside, and let God be God.

Listen to me carefully. The king couldn't stop the decree. Finally, the king had to have his friend thrown into the den of lions, and there in that den of lions, the Bible says he said to his friend Daniel, "Thy God whom thou servest continually, he will deliver thee" (v.16). We are talking about a pagan king who looked at the life of Daniel, and said, "Your God will deliver you," and by faith, took his friend Daniel, and had him thrown into the den of lions, sealed it with his signet, and they put a stone upon it, and the king went to his chambers. The Bible says he didn't eat, he wouldn't do anything, he fasted, and I believe, he prayed that night. This heathenistic king was praying, *"God, I don't know you, but if you are there, would you please spare my friend? God, I don't know you, but if you are there, please rescue Daniel. He's a good man. He is a man who loves you. He is a man who serves you."* I would like to have heard the prayer meeting that went on in that chamber. No music, no food, and that king fasted all night.

Then, came early morning. I believe just past midnight, he was on his way to the lion's den. The decree had been satisfied, the punishment had been completed after midnight. "I can go. It is the next day." He looked down, removed the stone, "And when he came to the den, he cried with a lamentable voice unto Daniel: and the king spake and said to Daniel, O Daniel, servant of the living God, is thy God, whom thou servest continually, able to deliver thee from the lions?" His faith was wavering. He was afraid. There were probably tears streaming down his cheeks. "O Daniel. I'm so sorry I threw you in there. "O Daniel, servant of the living God, is thy God, whom thou servest continually, able to deliver thee from the lions?"

"Then said Daniel unto the king, O king, live for ever. My God hath sent his angel, and hath shut the lions' mouths...." His angel. Do you see that? His angel. I believe that His angel doesn't just mean any angel. I believe His angel means the Angel of the Lord. I believe that angel in the lion's den was none other than Jesus Christ before we knew him as the virgin-born Son of God. The pre-existence, the pre-personification of the Lord Jesus Christ himself, that angel was. That angel came, and he shut the mouths of the lions, showing as a type of the future in which someday, there would come one born of a virgin. He, being sinless and pure, King of kings and Lord of lords, that Son, Jesus Christ, would come as not just our angel, but as the Creator of all angels. He would come, and shut the mouth of the lion for you. I like that, don't you? That is good.

Daniel says, *"My God hath sent his angel...."* I believe that is the angel of the Lord. Without getting into a lesson on theology, and the pre-existence of Christ, and all those things, I just want to put it plain — I believe Jesus Christ made a trip to the lions' den. We didn't know him as Jesus Christ, but he was in existence. He is God, himself. From everlasting to everlasting, the Son of God is God, and before anything was created that was created, Jesus is the Creator of the angels, higher than the angels. He is the Son of Almighty God, God in the flesh, the personification of Jehovah.

Now listen. Darius was the king who wanted to be God. Daniel was the servant, and we ought to be wanting to be just like him. The accusers told Darius that Daniel was praying, and there was not any way he could get around it, the king had to do what the decree declared. The accusers were nothing other than the buffets of Satan, himself. And then there are the lions, the tragedies of life, and the end of life, if we do not have the angel of the Lord, the Lord Jesus Christ, to intervene in our life.

First of all, I want to show you the king's decree. What was his decree? "You cannot pray to anyone but me. You cannot trust in anyone but me. You have to honor me." That was the decree of the king, and it could not be changed. I am going to make some statements, and I want you to take this in the spiritual. Grab this by the Spirit. Darius the king, who wanted to be God, is a picture of the heart of God without flaw or seam. Darius made a decree. Did you know that God made a decree, too? "The soul that sinneth, it shall die," (Ezekiel 18:4). Did you know that God so loved the world? Darius so loved Daniel? Did you know another King, who is King Jesus declared a decree and the decree was "The soul that sinneth, it shall die." The decree was "...whosoever was not found written in the book of life was cast into the lake of fire," (Revelation 20:15). The decree is "...whatsoever a man soweth, that shall he also reap," (Galatians 6:7). The decree is, that whosoever shall reject the Lord Jesus Christ, "the wrath of God abideth upon him," (John 3:36). That cannot be altered. The decree of God Almighty, the decree of King Jesus is, "The soul that sinneth, it shall die," and there is no other way under Heaven in which that decree is to be changed. It cannot be changed. That decree must be set in Heaven and earth forever. Darius couldn't change His decree, and there is something else. God couldn't change His decree either. He loved you, more than Darius loved Daniel. The King of kings, the Lord Jesus Christ, who is God, sought for a way to get around the decree, "The soul that sinneth, it shall die," and there was only one way to get around the decree. Someone had to die. And that someone did die. His name was and is Jesus Christ, and Jesus came and satisfied the demands of a holy God, and so satisfied the decree.

Now listen. No matter how hard God tries, He can't let sin get past him. It has to be judged. It is decreed that way. And no matter how hard God tried, he loved Daniel. He loves you. And no matter how hard King Jesus tries, the decree must be satisfied, so instead of Jesus being like Darius, Jesus said, "I'm not going to throw Daniel in there. I'm going in there myself. Hey, Daniel, stay home. I'll go down into the den of lions myself. Only this time, angels won't come, and shut the mouths." Read it for yourself. Psalms 22. Jesus went into the den of lions, and he was eaten up. He was crucified. He was put to death, to satisfy the decree of Heaven, The soul that sinneth, it shall die. Do you see it? Do you see the type and picture of redemption here? Isn't this beautiful!

The king makes a decree that can't be changed. King Jesus made a decree that couldn't be changed. Only, Darius chose to trust the living God of Heaven to deliver his servant Daniel. And this time, God himself said, "I'll trust no man." But God Himself steps from Heaven into the virgin womb of Mary, is conceived of the Holy God, God in flesh, and says, "I'll take care of the world. I'll take care of redemption. I'll go to the hungry lions.

So, we have Daniel the servant, and his accusers. Your biggest trouble will not be the drug pusher. Your biggest trouble will not be the bartender. Your biggest trouble will not be the sinful man or woman out in the world. As a child of God, your biggest trouble will be those who labor among you, those who are gathered with Daniel as the presidents and princes. Your biggest trouble will be in the very ones you rub shoulders with, the very ones you pray with, and the very ones you stand with. The biggest problem in all of church is not the outside. The devil can't hurt the church from the outside, but if he can get inside, and let one person begin to move about as a roaring lion, he can cause havoc in the house of God. And the devil knows that, so he accuses the brethren through people who are getting into a spirit of condemnation and criticism. And I want to say, don't be like the accusers of the brethren. Don't be like Satan. Back off. Pray three times a day to your God. Be committed to your God. Don't say anything negative about your brother and sister. Pray, and let God move in your life.

Darius was the king who wanted to be God, and he couldn't. Jesus is the King who is God, and took care of the problem. Now wait a minute. I want to make another statement. Darius really wasn't the king. He just thought he was. The king has always been Jesus. He is King of kings, and Lord of lords. And by the way, you need to get a glimpse and vision of Jesus Christ as King, and there is no other king, but the King of kings, the Lord Jesus Christ. If King Jesus is over all the other kings, that makes all the other kings nothing.

Darius wasn't really the king, so his decree wasn't all that important, except in the eyes of man. But the decree God made is all important, and King Jesus has made a decree, and he really is King. Here is the King's decree. "That at the name of Jesus every knee should bow, of things in heaven, and things in earth, and things under the earth; And that every tongue should confess that Jesus Christ is Lord, to the glory of God the Father," Philippians 2:10-11. "And my God has sent his angel," Daniel said. "My God has sent his angel to close the mouths of the lions." And Jesus, I believe, descended from Heaven into the midst of those hungry lions and he was there before Daniel ever hit the bottom, standing there, waiting on his servant to come. Jesus was already there, with the lions tied up and sitting over in a corner. *King Jesus descends into that hungry den of lions, and he says something maybe like this, "Here Kitty, Kitty, Kitty, Kitty."* See Jesus as Master. "Here Kitty, Kitty, Kitty." And he just shuts their mouths. Daniel falls in there, praying. What would have happened to Daniel if he hadn't been praying? He would have been eaten up. The time to pray is before you get there. He was prayed up. And by the way, if you get prayed up, you won't be eaten up by depression all the time. You stay prayed up, and you won't be eaten up with weakness all the time. If you stay prayed up, you won't be eaten up with anger, lust, or lasciviousness all the time. You won't be eaten up by the lions all the time. Stay prayed up, and King Jesus will be there, saying, "Here Kitty, Kitty, Kitty."

Whoever heard a sermon titled, *The King's Decree*? That sounds dignified, I know. But *Here Kitty, Kitty*, that is better. Get excited about Jesus. King Jesus made a decree, and here is the decree.

> **When thou passest through the waters, I will be with thee; and through the rivers, they shall not overflow thee: when thou walkest through the fire, thou shalt not be burned; neither shall the flame kindle upon thee.**
>
> **For I am the LORD thy God, the Holy One of Israel, thy Saviour....**
>
> **Isaiah 43:2,3**

Here is the decree. Every knee shall bow. Every tongue shall confess that Jesus Christ is Lord. Here is the decree. He that hath the Son hath everlasting life. Here is the decree. "For God so loved the world, that he gave his only begotten Son, that whosoever believeth in him should not perish, but have everlasting life," (John 3:16). Here is the decree. "…greater is he that is in you, than he that is in the world," (1 John 4:4). Here is the decree. "...the blood of Jesus Christ His Son cleanseth us from all sin," (1 John 1:7).

"Here Kitty, Kitty, Kitty. I'll knock your jaws off. I'll slap you so hard, you'll wish you never challenged a child of God. Here Kitty. I'll whip you so hard you will wish you were born a skunk instead of a lion. Come on Kitty." Greater is He that is in me than he that is in the world. "Come on Kitty. Hide and lurk under the bed in the darkness. Hide and lurk in the corner of darkness, with your beady eyes, Satan. I'll hit you so hard, you'll wish you could go to Hell sooner."

Do you see the beautiful redemption in this story? I've heard this story all my life. I've heard it in Sunday School, and it causes joy to fill my soul. I love to hear stories about Daniel, thrown into the den of lions, and God delivering him. I love David killing Goliath. He took that sling, and hit him right between the eyes with a stone, and big old Goliath goes, Kaboom! David walks up there, pulls the sword out of the sheath of Goliath, Goliath's own sword, and swish, takes his head off, reaches down and grabs the head of Goliath and walks across the field to Saul's office with that bloody head dangling from his hands. He slaps it across the desk of Saul and says, "Is this the man that troubleth Israel?" So you say, "It didn't happen like that." Well, I like it that way. "Preacher, that is gross." I would have mounted his head, that is what I would have done. Put it on the wall.

By the way, love restores, but God intends us to see that there was a king who made a decree. And he really was the King. He wasn't Darius the king who wanted to be God. He is the King who is God. God wanted us to see the King, the Lord Jesus Christ, who made a decree, and that decree was, "No man should have any other gods but me." No one was to bow to any graven image. Everyone should come to Jesus, "...for I the LORD thy God am a jealous God," (Exodus 20:1). "I'll have no other gods before me." God wanted you to see a king who is God, who made a decree that you cannot have any other gods, you can't worship any other gods, and that God is a jealous God. And if you go the way of worshipping other gods, you shall be thrown to the hungry lions, and Satan will destroy your soul. That is the decree.

Wait a minute! I'm not going to bow to idols. I'm not going to bow to the gods of man. I'm going to bow to King Jesus. And King Jesus, there is only one way to get around this. I can't stop the decree. It is written in Heaven forever. "For ever, O LORD, thy word is settled in heaven," (Psalm 119:89). Jesus says, "You just stay put there. I wasn't even born yet, so I'm not going to go anywhere yet. Just stay put there." And by the way, all of you weren't born then either, and you were going to stay put too. "Just stay put there. I'm going to go down there and go in the den of lions for you. I'm going to die for you." And by the way, the King who is God, signed a decree, which is the Bible, and it cannot be altered. It is forever settled in Heaven, and the soul that sinneth, it shall die, and God could not satisfy the holiness of himself. God could not stop the decree. It was forever settled. As much as he loved Daniel, as much as he loves you and me, God could not stop his own decree, that the soul that sinneth, it shall die, so God said, "I'll take care of this." And as Darius threw Daniel into the den of lions, trusting in the living God, God said, "I'll trust in no other. I swore by no other. I made an higher oath. There is no other place higher than I can swear, so I will swear an oath of myself. I am God. I, even I, am the Lord God, and you must come to me in order to be saved." That is the decree.

God said, "I'm not going to let anyone else take care of this. They will mess it up. I'll just take care of it myself." And there was a great turmoil in the heart of God, I don't know when. He is everlasting to everlasting. But before I was ever born, there was a great turmoil in the heart of God, and God said, "I loved you, before you were ever born." Before there was ever a blade of grass, God said, "I love you." Before God hung the heavens, before God ever made the planet earth, or made the mountains, or hung the sky or the stars, God said, "I love you." You didn't know it, but He loved you. And I don't know when it was, but God, at one time in eternity, just like Darius, could not sleep because he could not get out of the decree. And God said, "I know what I'll do. I'll go down and take care of the den of lions myself. Here Kitty, Kitty, Kitty." And he did. And King Jesus decreed,

> **That if thou shalt confess with thy mouth the Lord Jesus, and shalt believe in thine heart that God hath raised him from the dead, thou shalt be saved.**
>
> **For with the heart man believeth unto righteousness; and with the mouth confession is made unto salvation.**
>
> **Romans 10:9,10**

"Whosoever shall call upon the name of the Lord shall be saved," (Romans 10:13). That is a decree and declaration forever.

I can say to you, that every time a storm comes your way, Jesus says, "Here Kitty, Kitty, Kitty." "Master, carest thou not that we perish? The sea is raging. The waves are coming into the ship. Carest thou not that we perish?" So Jesus rises, and goes to the front of the ship, and says, *"Peace, be still."* Do you know what he was saying? *"Here Kitty, Kitty, Kitty. Shut up!"* Lazarus is dead. He stinks by now. It is too late. The stone is there. He is dead. Mary and Martha are crying, and the Bible says, *"Jesus wept,"* (John 11:35). Then he said, *"Roll away the stone."* Master, he stinketh by now. And the Lord of lords and King of kings made a decree that death no longer has any power over the resurrection, who is Jesus Christ, and Jesus said, "Here Kitty, Kitty, Kitty. *Roll away the stone. Lazarus, come forth."*

Kitty cats are for pulling whiskers. I love whisker pulling. If I see someone with whiskers, I want to pull their whiskers. I'm tempted to do it right now. If I go fishing and catch a catfish, I pull its whiskers. What is the use of cat-fishing if you can't pull its whiskers? But do you know what? When Daniel got into that den of lions, he didn't pull whiskers. I believe he didn't irritate them. But I believe when Jesus showed up, he pulled some whiskers.

Jesus is our Samson who rent the lion in two. Jesus is the Angel of the Lord who came, and shut the mouths of the lions where Daniel was. Jesus is the fourth man in the furnace of fire with Shadrach, Meshach and Abednego. Jesus is the Angel who stood with Abraham and said, "Your wife, Sarah, is going to have a baby." Jesus is the one who said, "Abraham, I'll make you a father of many nations." And by the way, in John 5, at that pool of Bethesda, where the angel that came down in the season and troubled the water and whoever stepped in first was healed, I believe that angel was Jesus. I believe He came down, and troubled the water, and whoever jumped in was healed. Only this time, the lame man who was laying there by the pool, met King Jesus who asked, "Wilt thou be made whole?" And he said, "Sir, I have no man when the water is troubled to put me in the pool. While I make my way to the pool, another steps in before me." And Jesus said, "Don't worry about the pool. Take up your bed, and walk." That is Jesus.

So next time the devil starts giving you a hard time, just say, "Here Kitty, Kitty, Kitty." Do you know what that means? If he is stupid enough to come to you, let him have it. But most of the time he will turn, and run as fast as he can go, because he heard some-one one time say, "Here Kitty, Kitty, Kitty," and he had the darkness beat out of him.

If I Go to Church, the Roof will Fall in!

Back when I was traveling in evangelism, I met a unique pastor in the foot hills of Missouri. He told me a story that goes like this: A special ladies choir came to his church for a musical. The choir director's name was Harry Leggs. Because the church was small, all the ladies were sitting in the auditorium. So, when it came time for the choir to sing, with a loud sounding voice, my friend who is the pastor said, "Now, will the ladies with Harry Leggs please come forward." With that, the crowd just roared with laughter.

Did I hear you say, "If I go to church, the roof will fall in?" Listen, if God wanted to get you, he could get you in the barroom, too. Now look! Let's talk. To some of you, church is a strange place.

> I read a story about a cowboy, from the pastor's story file by Michael Hodgin, in which the cowboy went to church for the first time in his life. He enthusiastically told a friend about his church experience. He recalled, "I rode up on my horse, and tied him by a tree in the corral." The friend said, "You don't mean corral; you mean parking lot." "I don't know, maybe that is what they called it," he said. "Then I went in through the gate." You don't mean the gate; you mean the front door of the church." "Well, anyway, a couple of fellows took me down the long chute." "You don't mean the long chute; you mean the center

aisle." "I guess that is what they call it. Then they put me in one of those little stalls!" "You don't mean a stall; you mean a pew!" "Oh yeah! Now I remember," said the cowboy, "That's what that lady said when I sat down beside her!" Now listen, cowboys are some of the cleanest people I know, and of course, this is just an old joke, but it does prove my point.*

The church is different than most places and rightly so. The church's ways, music, language, and atmosphere are different, but what you must remember is the church represents a different world. The church should be a reflection of heaven. But because the church is different, some are afraid to come. However, remember God loves you, and so do God's people. Don't stand on the outside of the church, the church is for you. It is made up of born again believers who are just cowboys, farm boys, factory workers, doctors, lawyers, plumbers, carpenters, etc. Oh, yes, one more word of instruction to the cowboy. If you do bring your horse, leave him outside, and if you have spurs, bring them in. The pastor could use them.

Treasures in the Snow

Snow — I know it's cold, wet, and nasty, and many times it can be a terrible road hazard. For those of us who drive, installing chains can become a nightmare, or at least a big hassle. But we all have to admit that snow is beautiful stuff. In Job 38:22, the Bible is asking the question "Hast thou entered into the treasures of the snow?" When I look at a fresh snowfall, I am reminded that God still speaks through His creation. Snow is His text, written in letters of white.

I am sure there are many spiritual lessons we can learn from the snow. However, let me suggest three beautiful pictures of the snow found in God's Word.

First, let us always be reminded snow is an awesome picture of God's power. In Job 37:5-7 it proclaims,

> **God thundereth marvelously with His voice; great things doeth he, which we cannot comprehend.**
>
> **For he saith to the snow, be thou on the earth; likewise to the small rain, and to the great rain of his strength.**
>
> **He sealeth up the hand of every man, that all men may know His work."**

Just think, *"For he saith to the snow, be thou on the earth."*

Think of the purity of snow, and how useful it is, soft and silent, yet powerful. It's truly silent power. I must confess, I find God's silent power working in my life, too. Nobody sees it, but it is producing beautiful things in my life. Today, others can see fruit in my life as a direct result of God's working power in my life.

This brings me to another great picture of snow, and that is our need. In Job 24:19, we find this great statement, "Drought and the heat consume the snow waters; so doth the grave those which have sinned." Just as the dry land needs the gentle snow waters, we too, need the spiritual waters of Heaven. Without God's blessings, our lives would be a barren, dusty desert. Of course, all thorns and thistles are a result of the fall of sinful man. Listen to what Jesus said to our dry, and thirsty souls. It's found in John 7:37,38, *"If any man thirst, let him come unto me, and drink. He that believeth on me, as the scripture hath said, out of his belly shall flow rivers of living water. (But this he spake of the Spirit)."* Now let me strongly point out, our need is life from above, not sin from beneath. When we look at the mountains, we are often reminded of their snow caps, which they have received from the heavens. Later, the snow will slowly melt, producing rivers and streams flowing perpetually into our valleys. I know of another mountain called Calvary, which is the precious Son of God who suffered and died for the cleansing of the world. Today, a stream flows from Immanuel's veins, for forgiveness and healing.

That brings us to another beautiful picture of the snow. Snow is a picture of forgiveness. In Psalm 51:7, sinful David cries out unto God, "Purge me with hyssop, and I shall be clean: wash me, and I shall be whiter than snow." God also speaks to us through the prophet in Isaiah 1:18, *"Come now, and let us reason together, saith the Lord: though your sins be as scarlet, they shall be as white as snow; though they be red like crimson, they shall be as wool."* Just think, scientists tell us that every grain of sand, every star, every blade of grass, every fingerprint, and every snowflake is different. Trillions have fallen, yet none are just alike, as if God is saying in every snowflake, "I will forgive."

Romans 5:1 declares, "We have peace with God through our Lord Jesus Christ." Hebrews 10:19 tells us that we can enter into the very presence of a Holy God by the blood of Jesus Christ.

Now as I close, let me remind you that God ever so sweetly wants to use His power to change your life, often silently within your heart. He will make you pure, and white as snow.

Before we are tempted to complain again about the snow, let us remember, it is the snow from above that makes things below much greener, and fruitful.

> **For as the heavens are higher than the earth, so are my ways higher than your ways, and my thoughts than your thoughts.**
>
> **For as the rain cometh down, and the snow from heaven, and returneth not thither, but watereth the earth, and maketh it bring forth and bud, that it may give seed to the sower, and bread to the eater:**
>
> **So shall my word be that goeth forth out of my mouth: it shall not return unto me void, but it shall accomplish that which I please, and it shall prosper in the thing whereto I sent it.**
>
> **Isaiah 55:9-11**

Eternity is Too Long to be Wrong!

Some speakers, and most listeners would approve of the rule among certain tribes in Africa. Their regulation is that when a man rises to speak, he must stand on one foot while delivering his speech. The minute the lifted foot touches the ground, the speech ends, or the speaker is forcibly silenced.**

Our life that God has given us is a wonderful thing. However, life as we know it today will someday come to an end. The other foot will drop, and we will then find ourselves face to face with God. My friend, Eternity is too long to be wrong. So let me be brief, but blunt. God's word declares in Hebrews 9:27, "And as it is appointed unto men once to die, but after this the judgment."

> Many years ago the popular preacher, Charles Spurgeon, was admonishing a class of divinity students on the importance of making the facial expressions harmonize with the speech in delivering sermons. "When you speak of Heaven," he said, "Let your face light up, and be shining with a heavenly gleam. Let your face shine with glory. And when you speak of Hell ... well, then your everyday face will do."**

I'm sure Mr. Spurgeon not only meant to be a little humorous, but also meant to be very realistic with his students. Life is tough, and only God can give you a little Heaven to go to Heaven in. If we are going to make Heaven our home, we must prepare to meet our God.

> My old pastor told of a hobo who knocked on a farmer's door, and asked for some food. "Are you a Christian?" asked the farmer's wife. "Of course," said the hobo. "Can't you tell? Just look at the knees of my pants, don't they prove it?" The farmer and his wife noticed the holes in the knees, and promptly gave the man some food. As the hobo turned to go the farmer asked, "By the way, what made those holes in the seat of your pants?" "Backsliding," said the hobo.**
>
> I'm afraid this light-hearted story reflects the spiritual condition of all too many good people. Good people who are just not ready to meet God. This story is about a man who was driving his car with his wife in the back seat. His car stalled on a railroad track. His wife screamed, "Go on! Go on!" The husband responded, "You've been driving from the back seat. I've got my end across the track. Now see what you can do with your end."**

The honest truth is most people are like a stalled car on the railroad track. Time is moving full steam ahead like a locomotive. However, there is no reason for any of us to be devastated, and condemned at the Holy Judgment Bar of God. My friend, don't let the devil convince you that all religious stuff is bad, and that no one really knows for sure there is a God and a final judgment. What if you're wrong? Eternity is too long to be wrong. Are you going to Heaven or to Hell? Are you going to be on the side of God or Satan? It is foolish and wicked to postpone the matter. If you have not personally trusted Christ, and do not know your sins are forgiven, then I beg you, turn your heart to Jesus Christ today, admit to Him that you are a sinner, ask Him to forgive you, and commit yourself to Him to be His forever.

> **For we must needs die, and are as water spilt on the ground, which cannot be gathered up again; neither doth God respect any person: yet doth he devise means, that his banished be not expelled from him.**
>
> **2 Samuel 14:14**

Remember, *"The wages of sin is death; but* (Praise God!) *the gift of God is eternal life through Jesus Christ our Lord,"* Romans 6:23.

Nobody's Going to Make a Christian Out of Me!

Years ago I heard about a Baptist and a Christian church that were trying to merge. All the members of both churches agreed, except one old-timer. "No way," he said as he shook his head. "Why, Sir?" he was asked. "Well, my mother and father were Baptists, my grandparents were Baptist, all of my people were Baptist — and nobody is going to make a Christian out of me now!"*

Now I know, and so do you, that religion is powerless to save. I'm aware that the sign above the church building only identifies the beliefs inside. However, I think it would be great if everyone in church, or out of church, would allow Jesus Christ to take full control of his life. Only Jesus Christ can make you a Christian when you repent of your sins, and turn to God. *The next few lines are very sad. Thus I approach them with fear and trembling, but perhaps it's needful to stir up one to repentance.* I would like to share a story I heard a few months ago. I believe this happened somewhere in Texas. There was a house on fire, and one little boy was caught in the upstairs. The fire chief reported that the little fellow had made his way to an open window, and climbed out on the roof. The firemen begged him to jump, but he was afraid. Finally, his daddy pleaded with him to jump into his arms, but the little fellow just couldn't get the courage to jump. He told his daddy he would find another way, and then crawled back into the burning house, never to return to his father's arms. Jesus said in John 14:6, *"I am the way, the truth, and the life: no man cometh unto the Father, but by me."*

My dear friend, there is no other way to escape the fires of Hell, except through the power of a Christ-like life. If you want a wonderful life, you must jump into the arms of God. Listen, there is nothing you are doing that is worth losing your soul over. Living for Jesus Christ is a wonderful adventure. It's unspeakable joy now and forever.

It's Your Move

Back when the automobile began to challenge the horse and buggy, my wife's dad told of an old man driving down a very narrow road with his buggy, and team of mules. Behind him came a teenager in his hot rod car. The teenager, no matter how hard he tried, just couldn't pass the team of mules. The road was just too narrow. However, when the road came to a cross section, the teenager, being very angry blocked the old man with his car, then jumped out with a pistol, and began shooting at the old man's feet saying, "Old man, can you dance? Hey, old man, can you dance?" The old man didn't say a word, he just walked up to his buggy, and mules, and pulled a double barreled shotgun out. Then he stuck the barrels up to the young man's nose, and said, "Young man, have you ever kissed a mule?" The young man replied, "No sir, but I've always wanted to."

Now the purpose of this message is not to hold you at gun point, or to pressure you — but I sure would like to see you filled with God's wonderful blessings. Did you know God is eager to hold you in his loving arms? Just look at this promise, *"Draw nigh to God, and He will draw nigh to you."*

A few months back I heard about a little boy, who after Sunday School, ran home as fast as he could, shouting breathlessly, "Mom, Mom, the preacher said, "If you draw a knife on God he will draw a knife on you!" Of course the preacher was preaching from a wonderful promise in the Bible found in James 4:8, "Draw nigh to God, and He will draw nigh to you." God tells us in a multitude of ways that if we will just respond to Him, He will, in return, respond to us.

God loves you so much that when you speak of him, or even think about him, He writes those beautiful memories of you in His own personal diary (Malachi 3:16).

When your heart is heavy, and your tears begin to drop silently on your pillow at night, God will put your tears in His Book of Remembrance. He then puts your tears in a special bottle (Psalm 56:8). Every prayer from your heart is kept in Heaven as sweet spices, and wonderful fragrances (Revelation 5:8).

Listen, when the devil tells you no one cares, and the circumstances look impossible, you remember God loves you very much, and there's not a tear, not a worry, and not one prayer that goes unnoticed by our omniscient God.

In Psalm 18, this whole song is filled with the little word "MY." This tiny word indicates possession, and often times expresses surprise, or pleasure. Just in verse two alone we find this tiny word "MY" eight times. "The Lord is MY rock, and MY fortress, and MY deliverer; MY God, MY strength, in whom I will trust; MY buckler, and the horn (power) of MY salvation, and MY high tower."

One can find personal pain in this Psalm, too. In verse six, the Psalmist declares, "In MY distress I called upon the Lord, and I cried unto MY God; he heard MY voice out of his temple, and MY cry came before him, even into his ears."

Hey, I've got some good news; when you're hurting, God sees and feels your pain, too.

It's your move. James 4:8, "Draw nigh to God, and he will draw nigh to you." First Samuel 2:30, "For them that honour me I will honour." Zechariah 1:3, "Turn ye unto me, and I will turn unto you." Malachi 3:7,"Return unto me, and I will return to you." Second Chronicles 15:2, "The Lord is with you, while ye be with him; and if ye seek him he will be found of you; but if ye forsake him, he will forsake you." Proverbs 8:17, "I love them that love me; and those that seek me early shall find me." Do you see it? You honor God, and He'll honor you. You turn — God will turn. You return — He will return. You come to Him — He will come to you. Do you remember the song — *"It's me, it's me, O Lord, standing in the need of prayer. Not my brother, not my sister, but it's me, O Lord, standing in the need of prayer?"*

Well, look around you. It's not your brother, or your sister, but it's you who needs to respond to God. The quality of your whole life, and future is in your hands, and the wisest thing you will ever do will be when you turn around, and place all you have in the hands of Jesus Christ. *There may need to be some strong changes made in your life. Perhaps some impossibilities stand in your way. Don't forget, it's still your move.* You want happiness? Start moving toward God, and his order for your life, and you'll find God's grace is manifold like the colors of a rainbow. Everyday is a new day with God. Your past may be a disaster, and your present may likewise be hideous, but the good news is your future is whiter than snow. *God is already there standing ready in your future to bless you.* Okay, just take this challenge. You do what you can do, and God will do what you can't do. IT'S YOUR MOVE! SHOW GOD TODAY YOU WANT HIS LOVING HANDS TO HOLD ALL OF YOU.

Come

Many four-lettered words spoken today are just a public announcement of a dirty heart. However, there are some wonderful four-lettered words such as love, hope, and life. *I think the queen of all Bible words is "Come."* Have you noticed "come" shines like the sun at the front and back door of the Bible? In Genesis 7:1 God said to Noah, "Come thou...into the ark." In Revelation 22:17, "The Spirit and the bride say, Come. And let him that heareth say *Come.* And let him that is athirst come. And whosoever will, let him take of the water of life freely."

"Come." My, what a fascinating, powerful word. Stop and think about it. It is one of the first words in man's vocabulary. Even a baby can understand its plea, and yes, a puppy or even a little kitten can comprehend its meaning. No wonder "come" is the queen of all Bible words. Listen to what Jesus said in Matthew 11:28: *"Come unto me, all ye that labour and are heavy laden, and I will give you rest."*

To the unsaved — Jesus cries, *"Come unto me, and have sweet rest."*

To the backslider — God cries, *"Come out of darkness and back to the light."*

To the lonely — He says, *"Come near to the very presence of God."*

To the fearful — He says, *"Come nigh."*

To the sinner — He says, *"I want all to come to repentance."*

To John on the isle of Patmos — He said, *"Come up hither, and see things that shall someday be."*

To Noah — He said, *"Come thou, and all thy house into the ark."*

To Zacchaeus — He said, *"Come down!"*

To the troubled disciples — He said, *"I will come again."*

On the sea — He said, *"Peter, come, and walk on the water to me."*

At the Rapture — He will say, *"Come up hither."*

To all nations — He invites, *"Come."*

When you pray — He says, *"Pray thy kingdom come, God's will be done."*

To the redeemed — He says, *"Come boldly to the throne of Grace to obtain mercy, and help in all times of need."*

To the church — He warns, *"I come quickly."*

To the weary — He invites, *"Come unto me."*

At the resurrection — He shall shout, *"Come forth."* And all that are in their graves shall come forth, some to resurrection of life, some to resurrection of damnation.

To the hungry — Come, all things are now ready. The Master's table is spread.

To the disciples — *"Come after me."*

To the doubter — Jesus says, *"Come, and see."*

To Parents — God commands, *"Suffer the little children to come unto me, and forbid them not."*

To the backslider — He says, *"Come home."*

To dead Lazarus — He cried with a loud voice, *"Come forth."* And out of the tomb he came.

To the cold, hungry, and defeated — God invites, *"Come, and dine."*

To the thirsty — He says, *"Come, and drink of the water of life freely."*

TO YOU — GOD INVITES, *"COME."*

Do You Have Unfinished Business?

Be Sure Your Sin will Find You Out!

In this book, I have shared with you a touch of humor, and some old-fashioned preaching. The following story was taken from Saratoga Press Publications, The Parables, Etc., by Michael Hodgin.

One winter day a man returned to his car from shopping at the local neighborhood mall. He smelled a rather rotten odor coming from under his car hood. He checked the engine compartment, and discovered a dead cat. It was rather mutilated from being caught in the fan belt. The stray cat had sought safety from the wind and cold, and didn't realize the dangers of resting on the warm engine block. The man proceeded to scrape, pull, and push the remains of the cat into a plastic bag. He closed the hood and went to wash his hands. As he was returning to get the bag from off the hood of his car, he saw a woman walk by, look suspiciously in both directions, grab the bag, and hurry off into the mall.

"Well, this is too good to be true!" The man thought as he laughed at what the woman had done. He decided to follow her and see what would happen next. She went into a restaurant and surveyed the bounty. She screamed and fainted when she looked into the bag. An ambulance was called and as she was about to be carried away, the man couldn't resist. "Hey, lady!" he shouted. "Don't forget your bag!"

And with that, he gently laid the plastic bag on the woman's chest just as the ambulance doors were closing.*

Have you ever heard the old saying "The cat's in the bag?" Of course, this means the truth has been discovered. *"Be sure your sin will find you out."* Numbers 32:23. Let me give you a little advice. Next time you think you've got the cat in the bag, check the bag. It may not be worth keeping.

When I have a broken tool, I go to find one that works. When I have a broken glass, I go find one that isn't. When I have a broken watch, I go purchase one that runs. So it is, when I find my decision maker broken, I go find someone else to make the right decisions for me.

My friend, by yourself there is no way you can find all the answers you need for your life. Especially, when sin hides in your every day life. Let God, and God's children help you through the maze.

It is a wonderful thing to attend the house of the Lord. There it is that we experience, and realize God's good pleasure. There it is that our soul is uplifted, and our mind is quickened in spiritual truth. Sunday is the Lord's day, and we would do well to begin it by making an effort to go to God's house to worship him. In fact, when we go, our fellowship, and faith in God is enlarged. Of course, there are also benefits offered by attending church. At church the soul can easily inquire of God's great blessings, and our fears can be stilled. Disappointments will fade away in the face of God's love. On the Lord's day our spirits can look away from the mundane world by being transported to the unseen world on the wings of faith. This special hour of worship is an hour when the heart stands still before God. The mind is quieted, and the Spirit is relieved of all anxiety. God's presence and companionship are evident.

Strength and rest are found in the rejoicing church. While casting all our cares upon Christ, we are relieved of heavy loads of frustration, distress and disappointment. To live without the love of God manifested in our life is not to live at all. Life is death unless the Holy Ghost encourages the mind, eases the heart of bitterness, and rids the soul of despairing thoughts.

As we walk with God, we are blessed, for God extends his mercy to us. He will reveal himself in countless ways. Deep within our hearts we will hear a sweet voice. This voice of God has the power to deliver; but, my friend, please take warning. There are other voices that are loud and persuasive. These are voices of a busy godless world. When we turn our hearts to Jesus, especially on the Lord's day, the voice of God is clearer than all. Our time spent in the house of worship will not easily be forgotten as we go about our daily task. The Christ of the sanctuary, the Lord of the temple, should be the Lord of the market place as well.

> **I was glad when they said unto me, let us go into the house of the Lord.**
>
> **Psalm 122:1**

> **Blessed are they that dwell in thy [God's] house; they will be still praising [God] thee."**
>
> **Psalm 84:4**

Let me close with this very important message to you from the Bible. It is found in Acts 2:36-47.

"Therefore let all the house of Israel know assuredly, that God hath made that same Jesus, whom ye have crucified, both Lord and Christ.

Now when they heard this, they were pricked in their heart, and said unto Peter and to the rest of the apostles, Men and brethren, What shall we do?

Then Peter said unto them, "Repent, and be baptized everyone of you in the name of Jesus Christ for the remission of sins, and ye shall receive the gift of the Holy Ghost.

For the promise is unto you, and to your children, and to all that are afar off, even as many as the Lord our God shall call.

And with many other words did he testify and exhort, saying, Save yourselves from this untoward generation. Then they that gladly received his word were baptized: and the same day there were added unto them about three thousand souls.

And they continued steadfastly in the apostles' doctrine and fellowship, and in breaking of bread, and in prayers.

And fear came upon every soul: and many wonders and signs were done by the apostles.

And all that believed were together, and had all things common;

And sold their possessions and goods, and parted them to all men, as every man had need.

And they, continuing daily with one accord in the temple, and breaking bread from house to house, did eat their meat with gladness and singleness of heart,

Praising God, and having favour with all the people. And the Lord added to the church daily such as should be saved.

I have no doubt, if you will be honest with yourself, you must admit church is a very important part of Christianity. If you have never asked Jesus Christ to become your Lord, if you have never repented of your sins, if you have never been baptized, or been filled with the Holy Spirit of God, if you do not belong to a local New Testament Church, then may I suggest you have some unfinished business to tend to.

The author acknowledges his indebtedness to the publishers and writers whose illustrations might apprear through right of public domain, or the principles of fair use. Songs referred to in this book are public domain. He further expresses his gratitude for the written permission granted from the following:

Some of the humor found in this book, coded with a double asterisk (**), is taken from: *Bob Phillips' Encyclopedia of Good Clean Jokes* by Bob Phillips. Copyright 1992 by Harvest House Publishers, Eugene, OR 97402 Used by permission.

The source of humor in this book coded with an asterisk (*) is from: *Parables, etc. and The Pastor's Story File* by Michael Hodgin. Copyright 1982-1995 by Saratoga Press PO Box 8 Plateville, Co. 80651 Used by permission. For additional humor call 1-888-785-2990 toll-free.

If you would like to contact the author,
you may write to:
Pastor James L. Eakins
PO Box 825
Ozark, Mo. 65721